Vital Signs

For Robert Wood Lynn

Contents

Preface

THIS BOOK is a product of a collaboration among the three of us which began in 1987. During these years we have learned much about mainstream Protestantism from one another and from many researchers, pastors, and lay people.

We prevailed upon many people to read the manuscript of this book, hoping that the resulting book would be a resource for large numbers of people in mainstream Protestant churches. In particular, we want to thank Nancy Ammerman, Dorothy Bass, Charles Brockwell, William F. Ekstrom, Darrell L. Guder, Steve Hancock, Dean R. Hoge, Robert W. Lynn, Jeffrey Myers, C. Ellis Nelson, George W. Newlin, Douglas F. Ottati, Amy Plantinga Pauw, Dorothy S. Ridings, Beverly Zink Sawyer, Andrew Scrimgeour, Thompson Smith, Carlyle Spohr, Barbara Wheeler, and James P. Wind.

A group of pastors in a D.Min. seminar read it carefully, and we appreciate their criticisms and suggestions. They are: Thomas Biery, Norwood Brown, David Feltman, William Haworth, Kay Huggins, Stanley Johnson, Scott Leslie, Gerald Little, David Massey, Craig Miller, Dan Mitchell, Edwin Peterson, James Reitz, James Spanogle, Peter Thompson, and Jeffrey Yergler.

None of the above friends and colleagues should be blamed for our errors or omissions.

William Hovingh and Deborah Prince gave us valuable assistance with references and helpful responses to our drafts.

We especially appreciate the support of the library staffs at Louisville Seminary, Western Seminary, and Union Seminary, as well as the support of our secretaries — Elna Amaral, Laura Graham, Kem Longino, and Jane Sutherland.

The patience of our families has been tested repeatedly during these eight years of endeavor, and we thank them for indulging our preoccupation with research and writing.

This volume is dedicated to Robert Wood Lynn, retired senior vice president of the Lilly Endowment. Not all of the research cited in this book came as a result of Lilly grants under Bob Lynn's tenure; but more than any single individual, his vision and grant-making have shaped what is now a sizeable and lively body of scholarship on American religion in the twentieth century. It was Bob Lynn who started the three of us down this path of inquiry, and we offer this book to him as a symbol of our gratitude for his friendship and for his contribution to the renewal of mainstream Protestantism.

Milton J Coalter
John M. Mulder
Louis B. Weeks

Introduction

IN THE late 1980s the three of us began an analysis of American Presbyterians as a case study of twentieth-century mainstream Protestantism. The results of the study eventually appeared in seven volumes as *The Presbyterian Presence*.[1] A vast amount of further research has enriched our understanding of the changes that have transformed American mainstream Protestantism.

The three of us have taught widely about this research, but we heard a common complaint in churches: "This material is overwhelming. The books are too long; the articles are inaccessible. Why can't you write something for the average person? Most important, can't we have something to use in an adult Christian education class?"

This book addresses that need. It summarizes the research on American mainstream Protestantism in the twentieth century and assesses the significance of that research for these denominations as they confront the twenty-first century. Our primary audience is church members and pastors or priests. We hope that this book will be a resource for congregations and denominations so that they might understand the trends of the past, the realities of the present, and the opportunities of the future.

Most importantly, we want to issue a word of hope to mainstream Protestants. The research has clearly demonstrated the complex challenges that confront them. In 1993 *Newsweek* chronicled

the travail of mainstream Protestant denominations under the head-
line, "Dead End for the Mainline?" — and the implied answer to
the question was clearly "yes."[2]

We disagree. Such obituaries, like Mark Twain's, are premature.
Despite their problems, these churches show "vital signs." We use
this terminology in two ways. First, we point to signs of vitality that
describe mainstream Protestantism in the present. Second, we suggest
how these churches might respond to their current situation. We offer
our proposals as potential sources of renewal that *prescribe* a course
of action leading to new vital signs in the future.

Mainstream Protestantism: What Is It?

The term "mainstream Protestantism" is sometimes confusing because it is used in several different ways. It first appeared during
the late fifties and early sixties. It has verbal cousins — "mainline
Protestantism," "liberal Protestantism," and "establishment Protestantism." Sometimes it is used to describe a particular group of
denominations, usually the American Baptist Church, the Christian
Church (Disciples of Christ), the Episcopal Church, the Evangelical
Lutheran Church in America, the Presbyterian Church (USA), the
Reformed Church in America, the United Church of Christ, and
the United Methodist Church.[3]

Since these denominations are affiliated with the National
Council of Churches, "mainstream Protestantism" sometimes
means conciliar Protestantism — though the NCC includes other
Christian bodies as well, such as the Greek Orthodox Church and
the major African American denominations.

"Mainstream Protestantism" is frequently used to refer to
religious groups that have exercised a dominant influence on American culture because of the size of their membership, or because of
the economic, political, and social prominence of their leaders and
members. When used in this way, and when focused in a particular
region, the term's scope can be broadened to include other denominations. For example, in the South, Southern Baptists could
be considered "mainstream" according to this definition.

"Mainstream Protestantism" also refers to a particular theological perspective in American Protestantism. This perspective has appreciated the tensions in the Christian gospel between grace and works, judgment and mercy, piety and intellect, and in being "in but not of" the world. In their better moments, mainstream Protestants have refused to collapse these tensions by refusing to stress one option to the exclusion of its counterpart. Instead they have measured their allegiances so that the gospel's tensions are preserved, although in unequal portions when the times demanded particular emphases. For this reason, mainstream Protestants have usually avoided rigidity in doctrine or practice. Socially, this tradition has accepted trusteeship for society and has used its power to shape American society and the world toward what it deemed to be constructive ends.

The ambiguous meaning of "mainstream Protestantism" creates problems. For example, some groups, like the Lutherans, were outside of the mainstream until the middle of the twentieth century.

Sometimes "mainstream Protestantism" is used to describe troubled denominations. Such institutions are afflicted by membership decline, institutional malaise, internal conflict, and theological confusion. Their loss of vitality, some suggest, means that "the mainline" has become "the old line" or "sideline."[4]

Some scholars object that there never was a mainstream in American religious history. They emphasize the extraordinary religious diversity of American culture, from the colonial period to the present day.[5]

Others protest that "mainstream Protestantism" suggests the religious and cultural superiority of denominations largely composed of white members of European ancestry. They argue that this use of the term ignores the fact that the Roman Catholic Church has been the largest Christian church in the United States for more than a century, or that the predominantly African American denomination, the Church of God in Christ, is larger than the Presbyterian and Episcopal denominations combined.[6]

For still other critics, "mainstream Protestantism" is objectionable for reasons related more to the future than the present or past. The use of "mainstream," they argue, fosters a dangerous and counterproductive nostalgia. The term suggests that these denominations' rightful place is in the center of American religious life. Accordingly, the solution to declining influence is for these denominations to recapture the power they have surrendered or have been forced to relinquish. The critics of this nostalgic solution, however, insist that faithfulness, not dominance or power, is the call of Christ to these denominations.

These criticisms of the term "mainstream Protestantism" are based on academic disputes about evidence, as well as ideological and ethical disagreements not only about America's religious past but also about its future. Like attempts to define and categorize other terms such as "evangelical," "fundamentalist," "conservative," and "liberal," our use of "mainstream Protestantism" is an imperfect way to refer to a complex set of institutions, values, traditions, and people.

Nevertheless, despite its difficulties and problems, we choose to employ "mainstream Protestantism" because it is more useful than alternative terms. We use it (1) to refer to the eight denominations mentioned above, (2) to describe part of American Protestant history, and (3) to describe a discernable theological commitment in American Protestantism. We believe that these eight denominations have exercised a significant, but not dominant, influence in American religion and culture.

Our definition of "mainstream Protestantism," therefore, is based on its institutional, historical, and theological significance, as well as on our belief in the tradition's persistent value. We are not prepared to abandon this tradition as a useful way of explaining part of America's past. Furthermore, we are committed to this tradition as a creative resource for understanding Christian discipleship in the future.

The Historical Context

As a background for understanding mainstream Protestantism in the twentieth century, we offer this brief outline of its historical setting.[7]

The Formative Period

From approximately 1740 to 1860, what later became mainstream Protestantism developed its distinctive characteristics and most of its institutions, programs, and values. This was the formative period of American Protestantism.

The majority of the features that developed in this formative period are so common today that we take them for granted. These include the separation of church and state, the formation of denominations, foreign and domestic missionary activity, Sunday schools, church related colleges and denominational seminaries, free will offerings as the means of financing churches, benevolent societies or what we know today as para-church groups, and the beginning of virtually the entire range of contemporary Protestantism's ethical agenda — including the issues of race, war, poverty, and gender.

For mainstream Protestants, an often proclaimed goal was "a Christian America," which meant a Protestant culture. Within these denominations, the most powerful movement shaping that vision was Protestant evangelicalism. In the late twentieth century, "evangelical" and "evangelicalism" refer to a particular branch of American Protestantism. During the nineteenth century, however, evangelicalism was embraced by virtually all Protestant denominations.

Nineteenth-century evangelicals stressed the necessity of a life-transforming experience of God's grace in Jesus Christ, the authority of the Bible, and the individual's mission to proclaim the good news of the Christian faith in both word and deed. Obviously, these Protestants differed enormously among themselves in how they worshiped, organized their denominations and churches, and understood the particularities of the Christian faith. But their lives were characterized by a common evangelical spirit or ethos, and they agreed that the newly independent American nation should be a Christian society (albeit defined in Protestant terms).

This attempt to forge a Christian society had obvious and serious flaws. To recognize the distortion of what was defined as "a Christian America," one need only look at slavery, the treatment of Native Americans, the legalized subjugation of women, or nineteenth-century Protestantism's virulent anti-Catholicism.

Nevertheless, these evangelical Protestants did succeed in creating a generally religious and specifically Protestant tone in many of American culture's institutions, laws, and customs. It was the power and persistence of these evangelical Protestants that made this formative period of American Protestantism so important in understanding mainstream Protestantism's problems and prospects in the late twentieth century.

The Critical Period

From the mid-nineteenth century to the early twentieth century, American Protestants encountered a series of challenges that make this epoch "the critical period" in their history.

New intellectual streams of thought raised troubling questions about Christian claims to truth. In the works of Darwin, Freud, and other scientists, psychologists, and sociologists, science challenged Christian understandings of the natural world and human nature. Biblical criticism questioned the historical accuracy of biblical narratives and raised anew the issue of biblical authority. The missionary movement made American Protestants aware of the complexity of world religions. As American Protestants became more aware of the pluralistic character of Christianity, the unique and authoritative status of Christianity itself was called into question.

These intellectual changes were accompanied by a transformation of American society. Immigrants streamed into the United States following the Civil War. They were "new" immigrants because they were primarily non-Protestant and non-English speaking — Catholics, Orthodox Christians, Jews from southern and eastern Europe and Asians from the Far East. America belatedly entered the Industrial Revolution, and the new immigrants provided a wealth of cheap labor. African Americans, who were concentrated in the rural South, sought new economic opportunities in cities, especially in the North. Immigration, industrialization, and urbanization changed the character of American society. No longer an agrarian, Protestant culture, America became an urban, pluralistic society in which large corporations and eventually strong government shaped communal life.

For mainstream Protestants, the goal of a Christian America remained the same, but they realized that they could no longer define that goal in exclusively Protestant terms. Now they shared religious authority with Catholics; and increasingly they recognized the need to respect and cooperate with Jewish people.

The Re-Forming Period

The "critical period" of the late nineteenth and early twentieth century was followed by an even more difficult period for mainstream Protestant churches. From approximately the 1930s to the present, mainstream Protestantism — in fact all of American religious life — has been redefined and restructured. What was "formed" during the formative period is being "re-formed" now.

The "re-forming period" and its changes are the subject of this book. During the twentieth century, mainstream Protestants have struggled to understand their relationship to other Protestants, to other Christians, and to the modern world. The challenges they have confronted have caused acrimony and division among these denominations, as well as between themselves and the society in which they minister. The changes within mainstream Protestantism have been far-reaching. Every aspect of the church has been affected — the nature of congregational life, the structures of denominations, theology and ethics, mission and outreach, worship and piety. The result is a new world — within the church and in society — for American mainstream Protestants.

Interpreting these changes is difficult. But among knowledgeable observers who seek to make sense of historical and contemporary trends, two alternative points of view are commonly proposed. One emphasizes the ascendancy and decline of various religious movements. There are "winners and losers," as one recent book argues. According to this view, American mainstream Protestantism is a "loser" in the competitive marketplace of American religion since it has declined in both numbers and influence.[8]

The other interpretation stresses change, rather than the rise and decline of groups, institutions, and religious traditions. This perspective recognizes both the persistence of religious institutions and their ability to adapt to new circumstances. What is important about mainstream Protestantism in American culture is not its decline but its changes and transformation.[9]

Our interpretation will draw on both of these perspectives, but we will accent a third perspective — the opportunities for renewal amidst decline and change. The vital signs of mainstream Protestantism exist not simply because of random circumstances or fickle popular will, but because mainstream Protestant visions of the Christian life, at their best, continue to illumine central insights into Christ's good news for human life.

After studying the research and after teaching hundreds of people about it, we also offer three perspectives on the current condition of mainstream Protestantism:

- The problems are not new.
- The problems are not unique to one denomination or a particular group of denominations, but affect all churches.
- The forces affecting American mainstream Protestant denominations also shape the rest of American culture.

Therefore, the beginning of wisdom is to distinguish between forces the church can affect and those it cannot.

This book is a focused case study of religious change in American culture. We hope it will illumine the vital signs of mainstream Protestants' history and their special vocation as Christians in the next millennium. We are convinced that the past cannot be recovered or recreated, but we are equally persuaded that these churches cannot confront their future effectively without knowledge of the past and the resources of the Christian tradition. As T. S. Eliot has written,

And whatever happens
began in the past
and presses hard on the future.[10]

Or, in the wisdom of the old proverb, "From the fires of the past, bring the coals, not the ashes."

1. A New World: Mainstream Protestants in the Twentieth Century

IN 1900, John R. Mott, the secretary of the Student Volunteer Movement for Foreign Missions, finished a tract for the times. Its famous title captured the optimistic, expansive spirit of American Protestants as they entered the twentieth century: *The Evangelization of the World in This Generation.*

The missionary movement, he wrote, "must ever be looked upon as but a means to the mighty and inspiring object of enthroning Christ in individual life, in family life, in social life, in national life, in international relations, in every relationship of mankind; and, to this end, of planting and developing in all non-Christian lands self-supporting, self-directing, and self-propagating churches which shall become so thoroughly rooted in the convictions and hearts of the people that if Christianity were to die out in Europe and America, it would abide in purity and as a missionary power in its new homes and would live through the centuries."[1] A tireless evangelist, Mott became an influential advisor to presidents and world leaders, crisscrossing the globe in pursuit of his vision.

As American Protestants approach the end of the twentieth century, it is clear that Mott's dream was both prophetic and flawed. Vast changes have transformed not only American Protestantism but also American Christianity — indeed Christianity across the globe. Mott's hope that Christ would be enthroned in every relationship of human life has been dashed by the barbarism and cruelty

1

of perhaps the most violent century in history. And yet, Mott's prediction about world Christianity was extraordinarily perceptive. As we approach the twenty-first century, it is clear that much of the Christian church's vitality is shifting from North America and Europe to Latin America, Africa, and Asia.

American mainstream Protestants now live in a new and different world. Many factors have affected the life of their churches. This chapter surveys eight of the most important developments that have shaped American mainstream Protestantism history in the twentieth century. These changes will also affect the future of churches in the third millennium of Christianity.

1. "The Third Disestablishment"

In 1993, Stephen L. Carter, a professor of law at Yale University, published an award-winning book with an arresting title: *The Culture of Disbelief: How American Law and Politics Trivialize Religious Devotion*.[2] The title spoke volumes about the altered state of religion in American society, particularly for American mainstream Protestants; only a century earlier a justice of the U.S. Supreme Court had declared the United States "a Christian nation."[3]

Although Carter focused primarily on U.S. legal decisions, his analysis explored a broader reality. American society is no longer supportive of religious ideas, Carter argued. It is now skeptical about the expression of religious belief. Other studies confirm this radical shift.[4]

This new environment was the result of an experiment launched by the founders of the American nation. In writing the Constitution, they separated church and state as legal entities and created the first secular state in the modern world. The ideal in Western Christianity for nearly 1,400 years had been an "established church" that supported the state while the state offered protection to the church. The United States decisively broke with that tradition through a legal "disestablishment." The drafters of the Constitution refused to grant privileged status to any church.[5]

As the largest religious group in the American population following the Revolution, Protestants resolved to use their strength in creating what amounted to a second establishment — "a Christian America." What they had lost legally they sought to regain religiously and culturally by shaping the laws, institutions, and customs of the nation on Protestant moral premises.[6]

Protestants frequently differed about what a "Christian America" looked like, and they changed their definitions throughout the nineteenth and twentieth centuries. They disagreed about slavery, the equal treatment of women before the law, and the use of war as an instrument of national policy, among other issues. Some causes attracted only transient ethical concern, such as cursing, dueling, or the delivery of mail on Sunday.

Behind the "Christian America" conceived by Protestants was a basic assumption that Protestantism's voice would be and should be heard by American society. That assumption was modified in the early twentieth century when Protestants had to share the podium with Roman Catholics and Jewish people. This shift became Protestantism's "second disestablishment."[7]

By the end of the twentieth century, a more profound change has occurred. Neither Protestants nor Catholics nor Jews — nor any of the other many religious traditions in American culture — can claim that their particular voice has the exclusive privilege of being heard and observed.

The result has been a "third disestablishment." The first was a legal disestablishment, separating church and state. The second was a religious disestablishment, in which Protestants had to share religious authority with Catholics and Jewish people. By the 1990s, American religious groups had experienced this third disestablishment, in which all religious bodies have been not only separated from cultural reinforcement and support, but in some cases actually suffer disadvantages.[8]

This cultural change is more obvious in some regions than others. For instance, it is most pronounced in the West and least obvious in the South. We met a man in Tupelo, Mississippi, who had recently moved from Westchester County, outside of New York City. When asked why he became a member of the Presbyterian Church, he explained that at first he had tried to find Sunday golfing partners. "I simply couldn't get a game on Sunday morning," he confessed. "Finally, I gave up and went to church along with everyone else."

In contrast, parents in other parts of the nation complain that junior high and senior high athletic events are scheduled on Sunday mornings — in direct conflict with their congregation's worship services. They find themselves battling and negotiating for their children's time, and the schedule is often determined by priorities that do not include participation in the church.

For adults, church attendance and membership are increasingly a matter of choice, rather than an expected or encouraged pattern of behavior. The church is one option among many for support or for the use of one's time. Contemporary American culture provides little encouragement to make the church a priority.

The third disestablishment in America has come as a shock to mainstream Protestants, especially because they had affirmed so much of American culture. When this culture became apathetic or hostile toward religion, mainstream Protestants found themselves adrift. One pastor captured it well when she reflected on the depth of commitment in her congregation: "You can't assume anything anymore."

Cultural disestablishment is one of the central and difficult realities confronting mainstream Protestants, and all other religious groups in American culture. What has been lost cannot be reestablished. But cultural disestablishment also offers a distinct opportunity for mainstream Protestants — an opportunity to develop and recover distinct and unique ways of being Christian that will win the allegiance of the church's members, not by cultural reinforcement, but by the power of its truth.

2. "Politicized" Religion

The Christian church, throughout its history, has always been involved in politics. Yet this concern for the political order has been influenced by several developments in the United States during the twentieth century.

One major factor has been the belief that government is a positive force for social change. Such belief began with the Populist and Progressive movements of the late nineteenth and early twentieth centuries, and has been reinforced by strong governmental initiatives ever since.[9]

As government expanded its role in American life, Protestants vigorously debated whether the church should be involved in politics. Early in the twentieth century Walter Rauschenbusch proposed *A Theology for the Social Gospel* (1917). His was not only a pioneering effort to adapt Christianity to the pressing needs of an industrial society, but also a defense of the church's support of a powerful nation-state. Others disagreed with this reform program and questioned the wisdom of the church's intervention in politics at all. The church, they argued, should confine itself to the private sphere — to the individual spiritual lives of its members. Still others maintained that one of the priorities of the church was the training of individuals for political life as responsible citizens; the church itself, however, was to exercise restraint in entering the political fray.[10]

A second important factor in this trend toward politicized religion was the increasing intervention of the courts into American religious life. Beginning in the 1940s and escalating after 1960, court cases involving the relationship of church and state redefined the role of religious institutions in American society. Despite considerable religious conflict earlier in American history, church-state litigation proliferated only in the mid-twentieth century. Furthermore, the courts accepted more responsibility for trying to resolve complex moral and ethical problems, such as abortion and euthanasia.[11]

The result has been politicized religion and politicized religious institutions. The power of government and the expanded scope of its activity have heightened the political awareness of all churches — conservative and liberal.

The political transformation of American culture in the twentieth century and the implications of that transformation for mainstream Protestants can be clearly illustrated by their use of mass media. In the early years of radio and television, the mainstream Protestant denominations enjoyed free programming. The national broadcasting networks provided the air time to ecumenical organizations, such as the Federal Council of Churches (FCC) and the National Council of Churches (NCC). Since federal regulations required networks to provide free public service programming, the FCC and the NCC, along with representatives from the Catholic and Jewish communities, were selected to satisfy the regulation. One of the signs of the cultural recognition of mainstream Protestantism, Catholicism, and Judaism was the privilege of free access to the nation's airwaves.

In the 1960s, the Federal Communications Commission, partly under pressure from evangelical Protestant groups, reduced the requirement for public service programming and allowed the networks to charge for air time. The mainstream Protestant churches of the NCC generally refused to pay the huge expense. In the meantime, conservative Protestants continued to pay and eventually dominated religious radio and television programming.[12]

Mass media are a prism for understanding the different context for the church and other religious institutions in American culture. The vast majority of Americans are now exposed to network programming that ignores religion, or treats it lightly as a factor in cultural life. The influence of religious institutions and values on the media has clearly declined. Although mainstream Protestants have not disappeared from the airwaves, Protestant programming is supported and produced mainly by conservatives.[13]

This new politics has been unsettling for many mainstream Protestants, particularly those who have looked to public institutions to support and reinforce religious, if not Christian, values. In addition, mainstream Protestants have generally endorsed the positive role of government. But as government policies and laws become increasingly neutral and occasionally hostile to religion and religious institutions, mainstream Protestants can no longer regard government as the ally they formerly relied upon. The intrusive power of the state, moreover, raises questions about the beneficial effects of governmental intervention. Like other religious groups, mainstream Protestants are left with little choice but to recognize the new politics of American society and to espouse a "politicized" religion.

3. Christianity as a World Religion

The twentieth century brought a revolution in Christianity. It has become a world religion. Initially based in the Mediterranean world, its strength for centuries was Europe and later North America. Because of the missionary movement of the nineteenth century and the growth of indigenous churches in the twentieth century, the Christian church has now expanded to every continent of the world. In the twenty-first century, Christianity's greatest numerical strength will be in Latin America, Africa, and Asia.

Statistician David Barrett charts the trends in the world Christian population. He estimates that the percentage of people in the world who had never heard the Christian message declined from 48.7 percent in 1900 to 20.6 percent in 1994. If present trends continue, he projects that only 7.1 percent of the world's population will not have heard the gospel by 2025.

The growth of the number of professing Christians in North America during the twentieth century has been impressive. According to Barrett, the number increased from 59.6 million in 1900 to 200.2 million in 1994, and he expects there will be 225.6 million in 2025.

The growth of Christians in Latin America, Africa, and Asia is even more dramatic. In Latin America in 1900, there were 60 million Christians, about the same as in North America. In 1994 the number had ballooned to 443.5 million, more than twice that of North America, making Latin America the most populous Christian continent in the world. By 2025, Barrett projects a total of 675.2 million Christians in Latin America.

But Africa seems to be the emerging stronghold of Christianity in the twenty-first century. In 1900, Barrett estimates, there were 8.8 million Christians in Africa. By 1994, the Christian population had increased to 296.3 million. By 2025 Africa will surpass Latin America with an estimated 760.1 million Christians, more than three times the estimated number of Christians in North America.

In East Asia, the number of Christians increased from 1.8 million in 1900 to 112.2 million in 1994, and is expected to increase to 230.4 million in 2025. In South Asia, the comparable figures for the Christian population are 16.3 million in 1900, 152.3 million in 1994, and 327.2 million in 2025.[14]

It is impossible to confirm the reliability of Barrett's statistics, but the trend is clear: the numerical strength of Christianity is

moving away from the north to the southern and eastern areas of
the world.

What this will mean for American mainstream Protestants and
for Christianity is unknown, but several implications are already
obvious. First, much of the Christian growth has and will come in
the pentecostal/charismatic tradition, with which American mainstream Protestants have often been uncomfortable. Barrett estimates that there were only 3.7 million pentecostal/charismatics in
1900; their ranks grew to 446.5 million by 1994, and will exceed
1.14 billion by 2025.[15] American mainstream Protestants will need
to expand both their understanding and appreciation of this powerful movement which is transforming world Christianity.[16]

Second, the growth of Christianity outside the West has already raised questions about Christian doctrine, which for centuries
has been understood in Western philosophical terms. Basic Western
ideas about God, human nature, history, and salvation may not be
readily transferrable to non-Western cultures. The result of this
difficulty will be a new and challenging theological diversity within
the global Christian church.[17]

Third, the expansion of Christianity into other parts of the
world will raise even more poignantly the question of the uniqueness of Christianity and its relationship to other religions. Also,
because of the growing migration from the Middle East, North
Africa, and Asia, Christians in the United States will increasingly
encounter people of other faiths in their own communities.[18]

4. Ecumenism

One of the fascinating results of the missionary enterprise of the
nineteenth century was the ecumenical movement of the twentieth
century. The difficulty of explaining differences among Christians
to non-Christians and the need to cooperate in missionary activity
produced new levels of mutual understanding and common work
among various Christian traditions. Ecumenism was described by
Anglican Archbishop William Temple in 1944 as "the great new
fact of our era,"[19] and it has transformed American Protestantism
and world Christianity.

Among American mainstream Protestants, the ecumenical movement is usually associated with institutions such as local councils of churches, the National Council of Churches, and the World Council of Churches. However, comparable associations exist for conservative Protestants as well. They include the National Association of Evangelicals, the International Congress on World Evangelization (sometimes referred to as the Lausanne Conference), the Christian Holiness Association, the Pentecostal Fellowship of North America, and a host of other associations focused on doctrines or particular issues.[20]

The most dramatic example of ecumenism in the twentieth century has been the rapprochement between Roman Catholics and Protestants — the result of the Second Vatican Council.[21] From the sixteenth to the twentieth centuries, Protestants and Catholics frequently defined themselves in terms of what they were not. As recently as seventy-five years ago, few devout Methodists would accept the premise that a Catholic could be a good Christian, and the same would have been true of most Catholics' verdicts of Methodists. Those attitudes changed — within one generation — especially in the United States.

Perceptions of Judaism also shifted. The holocaust of World War II made Christians keenly aware of the persecution of the Jewish people, as well as the Christian complicity in that horror. In the mid-sixties, Vatican II absolved the Jewish people of the responsibility for the death of Jesus, the first such action by the Roman Catholic Church in Christian history. In both theology and in practice, many American Christians increasingly respect Judaism and refrain from seeking Jewish conversions to Christianity.[22]

Ecumenism in the twentieth century has had mixed success. On the one hand, it has vastly improved relations among certain groups of Protestants, between Protestants and Roman Catholics, and between Christians and adherents of other religions. American mainstream Protestants now draw heavily on the worship traditions of other Protestants, of Catholicism, and occasionally even of Judaism. As an idea, ecumenism has triumphed. A recent poll demonstrated that Americans believe that religious differences are basically various and equal ways of finding God.[23]

In addition, community ministries flourish in both urban and rural areas. Sponsored by ecumenical alliances of congregations, these organizations provide services and ministries no single congregation could afford to offer. As a form of local mission, ecumenism is alive and well.

On the other hand, ecumenism has largely failed as a movement for organic union. There have been some notable denominational mergers among Lutherans, Methodists and Evangelical United Brethren, Presbyterians, and the Congregationalist Christians and Evangelical and Reformed, but the dream of a unified Protestant or Christian church has languished. The Consultation on Church Union (COCU) is a case in point. Launched by Episcopal Bishop James Pike and Presbyterian Eugene Carson Blake in 1960, it attracts little enthusiasm and support from mainstream Protestant denominations, even though it has abandoned its vision of institutional church union. Ecumenical organizations also suffer from lack of support. Local councils of churches, the National Council of Churches, and the World Council of Churches are all severely reduced in size and function.

In addition, the triumph of ecumenism as an idea has weakened commitment to particular Christian churches and eroded denominational distinctiveness. Like most American Christians, American mainstream Protestants do not believe there is any significant difference between different churches. They therefore feel free to transfer their religious loyalties as circumstances change.

The results of ecumenism are ambiguous. On the one hand, it has contributed to the declining significance of denominationalism by reducing the importance of the distinctive theological characteristics in various traditions. In doing so, ecumenism weakened a central motivation for individuals' commitment and allegiance to a particular church. On the other hand, ecumenism helped Christians look beyond the boundaries of ethnic ties, cultural habits, and denominational idiosyncracies. In this positive light, ecumenism represents in both theory and practice one of the most inspiring examples of Christian aspirations to embody the wideness of God's mercy.

5. The Fundamentalist Schism

In sharp contrast to the vision of unity in ecumenism, fundamentalism has played a major role in dividing American mainstream Protestantism during the twentieth century. In fact, no Protestant denomination has been left unscathed by fundamentalist controversies. In addition, the term "fundamentalism" is now being used to refer to radical, aggressive, or conservative movements within any religious community, including those outside of the Protestant or Christian tradition.[24]

Fundamentalism is characterized primarily by its attempt to define Christian doctrine precisely, as well as its militant opposition to different religious and cultural points of view. Although they share similarities, fundamentalism and evangelicalism are different forms of conservative Protestantism. (See chapter 4 for a more extensive discussion of fundamentalism and evangelicalism.)

Within both scholarship and the popular mind, fundamentalism has often been disdained or ridiculed. When it began to cause public controversy during the 1920s, H. L. Mencken sarcastically observed that all you need to do is "heave an egg out of a Pullman window and you will hit a Fundamentalist almost anywhere in the United States today."[25]

Recently, however, scholars have taken fundamentalism seriously as both a religious and a social movement. These scholars stress that fundamentalism is not a transient phenomenon which will eventually disappear. Rather, fundamentalism is a continuing religious option for people responding to fragmentation in the modern world. While social class and education are important elements contributing to the dynamics of fundamentalism, it cannot be reduced merely to sociological categories. Its religious character is crucial, for fundamentalism represents an assertion of certainty and clarity, as well as a protest against the ambiguities and relativism of modern life.[26]

Within American mainstream Protestantism, fundamentalist controversies have often produced schisms which led to the formation of new denominations. Because of their militancy and their desire for doctrinal precision and purity, fundamentalists are frequently separatists, citing 2 Corinthians 6:17 as their authority:

"Therefore come out from them, and be separate from them, says the Lord, and touch nothing unclean; then I will welcome you."

However, not all fundamentalists are necessarily schismatics, and not all conservative Protestants are fundamentalists. In fact, a major theme of Protestantism in the twentieth century is the acrimonious battle between conservatives and their more liberal opponents within denominational groups. Divisions *among* denominations have now become less significant than divisions *within* denominations. For example, conservative Episcopalians have more in common with conservative Methodists than with liberal Episcopalians. As churches increasingly responded to the growing and intrusive power of the state, and as politicized religion became characteristic of nearly all churches, social and political issues have further complicated the theological debates within each denomination.[27]

The result, argue James Davison Hunter and others, may be a series of "culture wars," waged within American culture.[28] Each denomination's fracas, as intense as it may be, is a microcosm of a larger "struggle for America's soul," according to Wuthnow.[29] The debates also illustrate the adage that politics makes strange bedfellows; for example, conservative Protestants have formed alliances with Roman Catholics and Mormons to oppose abortion.

Amidst the intensity of the internecine struggles over fundamentalism, liberals and conservatives have forged their identities over against one another. This left both movements ill-equipped theologically to articulate what it means to be Christian — as opposed to articulating "why I am not a liberal," or "why I am not a fundamentalist." One of the critical questions for American mainstream Protestants in the next century is whether they will continue to let the fundamentalist division define their theological and denominational future.[30]

6. Pluralism

E pluribus unum — "one out of many" — is the motto emblazoned on the national seal. From the colonial era to the present, pluralism is part of the fabric of our nation's history. Pluralism has at least two significant meanings when used to refer to twentieth-century American religion: one concerns ethnicity and gender; the other concerns truth and values.

The first meaning refers to the diversity of ethnic groups represented in the American population. The United States is the most ethnically diverse nation in the world. Given the ethnic and religious violence in other areas of the globe, it is astonishing that American history has not seen more violence between ethnic and religious groups, especially in this century.

In addition, the pluralism of the American people will increase, rather than decrease, during the twenty-first century. Hispanics and African Americans are the most rapidly growing ethnic groups in the United States. In Holland, Michigan, where the population had been mostly Dutch Calvinist for more than a century, Hispanic people constituted 17 percent of the population in 1990, and nineteen different languages were spoken by children in the public school system. If current trends continue to the middle of the next century, white people will be a minority in the United States, and Hispanic people may well be the largest single racial-ethnic group.[31]

The growing diversity of the American population is a challenge for mainstream Protestant denominations. With the exception of the American Baptist Church — which draws 27 percent of its members from racial ethnic minority groups, and with which many African American congregations have dual affiliation[32] — all of the mainstream Protestant churches are overwhelmingly white. In practical terms, these churches must diversify their membership in order to maintain present membership levels, and especially if they wish to grow. Most importantly, embracing greater diversity moves the church toward realizing the inclusive character of the body of Christ, as envisioned by the apostle Paul.

Women represent another symbol of diversity in mainstream Protestantism, and challenge the largely male character of church leadership and power. As early as the late seventeenth century, women members formed the majority in Protestant churches in America. During the nineteenth century, they achieved new power and recognition within Protestant denominations, largely through volunteer activity, mission work, and the funding of missionary endeavors. In the twentieth century, mainstream Protestant denom-

inations gradually changed their constitutions to enable women to
hold elected office and to be ordained as lay leaders and ministers.
By the late twentieth century, mainstream Protestant denominations have become distinctive in American Christianity for the
degree to which women participate in church leadership and shape
church vision.[33]

Pluralism — when defined as the sharing of power and influence among white males, racial-ethnic minorities, and women —
has become a significant factor in late twentieth-century mainstream
Protestantism. But pluralism becomes a more difficult challenge for
mainstream Protestants in this century when defined according to
its second meaning: the diversity of truth and values. Obviously,
racial-ethnic minorities and women may emphasize various aspects
of the Christian faith, and the church is enriched by this pluralism.
Mainstream Protestantism, with its theological commitment to a
central core of doctrine and practices, is willing to tolerate a limited
range of possible interpretations of the Christian tradition. This
tolerance of diversity sets mainstream Protestantism in sharp contrast to fundamentalism, with its insistence on precise doctrine.[34]

As liberating as this toleration can be, it nonetheless raises
significant problems for mainstream Protestant churches. Doctrinal
boundaries are blurred; the blending of other values within the
Christian faith becomes not only an option but an appealing alternative. For example, one poll revealed that 21 percent of mainstream Protestant church-goers believe in reincarnation, a belief
contrary to the Christian tradition.[35]

Equally important, pluralism of ideas raises the perplexing
question of authority in Christianity. Research indicates that American mainstream Protestants easily accept the idea that truth is
relative to different historical times and cultures. They have difficulty describing an authority for truth other than the one which
"works" for them.[36]

Pluralism of belief and practice within the church has been
and will become even more poignantly a challenge for mainstream
Protestants. But the diversity of Christianity itself will be less difficult to resolve than the larger question posed by Pilate to Jesus:
"What is truth?" (John 18:38).

7. Choice

Students of American culture have always noted the role of choice or voluntarism in American religion. The United States is, after all, a nation of religious freedom. Neither church nor state can dictate what people must believe. An American has both freedom *of* religion and freedom *from* religion.

Americans exercised that freedom throughout the colonial period and the nineteenth century, and most often they chose not to be members of churches. Despite the presumed religiosity of colonial Americans, only 5–10 percent of the population belonged to a church. The percentage had increased to 26 percent by the Civil War, 46 percent by World War I, 57 percent by World War II, and 69 percent by the late 1980s.[37]

Choice was less of a threat for established churches because they relied upon legal or cultural reinforcement of religious behavior and belief. But each successive disestablishment in American history posed the problem of how churches could maintain the loyalty and allegiance of their members. First the legal system and then the culture ceased to encourage Christian or religious values.

At the end of the twentieth century, choice has become an especially powerful impulse within mainstream Protestantism and American religious life. People choose whether or not to go to church. They choose the kind of church that appeals to them. They choose what to believe. They choose where to contribute financially. The majority of mainstream Protestants did not grow up in the denomination that they joined as adults. "Switching" — changing denominational allegiances — prevails.[38]

The prevalence of choice poses an especially significant challenge to mainstream Protestants. Obviously, a church is better off when people choose to become members rather than join because of family pressures, peer pressure, or social convention. Since American mainstream Protestant churches are not strict or rigid in their expectations for membership, they make it easy for people to enter the church. But if it is easy to join a mainstream Protestant church, it is easy to leave it as well.[39]

Choice also leads many to select a congregation because of its "compatible style." In the worst of cases, this means a congregation that does not challenge one with those parts of the gospel that are unsympathetic to an individual's current views or life style.

Toleration and pluralism are among mainstream Protestantism's most appealing virtues. They also represent its unique predicament of maintaining the integrity of the Christian faith, especially in a culture in which choice is so powerful.

8. The Declining Significance of Denominationalism

The denomination is a religious institution that was invented in America. It has now been exported throughout the Christian world. As a theological idea, it was a startling innovation in the history of Christianity. Denominationalism assumes that there is an irreducible Christian core. But some variety of belief and practice can exist among different churches, and all of them will be "denominated," or called "Christian."[40]

Denominations thrived in the American setting, particularly because of religious freedom, but also because of religious conflict. By the 1990s, there were more denominations than when the century began. In one sense, denominationalism has never been stronger.

Nonetheless, one of the significant factors shaping American mainstream Protestantism at the end of the twentieth century is the diminished power of denominations. Numerically, these denominations are declining in size. They no longer exercise the same influence in business, government, and education. Their members have accepted the ecumenical premise that denominational differences and theological traditions are insignificant. People therefore move freely from one denomination to another. As organizations, denominations are severely affected by the distrust and suspicion between congregations and national church structures. Congregations have become the center of power in every mainstream Protestant denomination.[41]

Why and how this happened, and what it means for mainstream Protestants, are questions about a complex set of forces that have affected nearly every American institution — from the corporation to the school board. Denominations will not disappear; they will continue to be, as historian Sidney Mead called them, "the shape of Protestantism in America."[42] But in the future, denominations will clearly be new institutions, with a different set of characteristics than they have had. Indeed, part of the genius of denominations has been their capacity to adapt and change.

*   *   *

At the end of a class session that explored this research on mainstream Protestantism, a perceptive participant captured the problem which many see when confronted with this information. Frowning, she asked, "Why is it so difficult to be a Christian today?"

It has never been easy to be a Christian. But beneath all the challenges described in this chapter lies that same gnawing question: Why is it so difficult to be Christian, particularly the kind of Christian represented by mainstream Protestants?

Many sociologists explain this difficulty by arguing that American society is becoming more secular. That may be partly true. But what perplexes these sociologists, and anyone else who looks closely at late twentieth-century America, is the persistence and vitality of religion, not its demise.[43]

Modernization theory is more helpful for understanding religion in American culture, and particularly helpful for understanding American mainstream Protestantism. As societies modernize, they divide life into discrete units. Society becomes fragmented: work, family, play, religion — all become distinct areas with little overlap or relationship with one another. This helps explain why some areas of society — such as education or the media — can be very secular and why religion and religious institutions still thrive. In modern societies, as one book title described it, people live with "homeless minds."[44]

In modern societies, those religious groups that define themselves distinctly and set themselves in contrast to the surrounding culture will thrive. They will thrive precisely because they accept the necessity of becoming a social fragment — a righteous remnant, perhaps. In contrast, the difficult challenge for mainstream Protestants has been and will continue to be their willing acceptance of the value of modern culture, even and especially because of its secular character, and their refusal to see life in fragmented terms.[45]

Nonetheless, mainstream Protestantism cannot restore the unity to human life. In fact, historian Martin E. Marty argues that the twentieth century has witnessed an increasing power of centrifugal forces in both religion and politics. Single issue groups — those divided by race, gender, age, and class — mark the life of denominations and society.[46]

But one of the most significant vital signs in mainstream Protestantism, one that is often overlooked, is its theological rejection of fragmentation in the modern world. In their reluctance to give up the quest to see the world as God has intended it to be, mainstream Protestants continue to express an eloquent Christian truth: the world was created good and has been redeemed in Jesus Christ. By refusing to withdraw from the world or compartmentalize religious faith, they engage the complexities of culture with the conviction that God's love and redemption in Jesus Christ will transform both them and the creation itself. This theological impulse has been central to mainstream Protestants' Christian identity, and it is a distinctive resource for their proclamation of the gospel in the next century.[47]

2. Changing Members, Changing Churches: Mainstream Protestant Membership Growth and Decline

DURING the last thirty years, mainstream Protestantism has been transformed by a dramatic loss of members. Although church membership has fluctuated throughout American history, never before has there been such a steep decline. From the mid-1960s to the mid-1990s, mainstream Protestants lost between 20 and 30 percent of their members, while membership in many conservative and fundamentalist churches gained in numbers each year.

Until the 1980s, this loss of members attracted little attention from scholars, the media, or even the churches themselves. In working with many congregations that experienced significant decline, as well as with the governing bodies of those congregations, we found that few seemed concerned. At one men's meeting, for example, fifteen elderly participants rattled around in a cavernous church building. On the wall were pictures of previous gatherings of a hundred and more men. We asked, "What are you doing to attract new members?" The president of the group gave a memorable reply: "We don't have to attract them. They just come."

In growing congregations, the members are often upbeat and optimistic. They find it difficult to believe that their denomination has significantly declined in membership. An expanding suburban church full of young parents and committed leaders invited one of us to preach on a Sunday when three infants were baptized and three adults were received by baptism and profession of faith.

19

"We're gaining members at a rate of about one hundred a year," the pastor explained.

Despite the denial of membership decline, the loss in numbers was and is real. As early as 1979, Martin Marty declared that a "seismic shift" was occurring in American religion.[1]

The Christian Church (Disciples of Christ) has fared the worst overall. Losing members as early as 1955–60, and as many as 25 percent during the period from 1965 to 1970, the Disciples of Christ continued during 1985–90 to lose a higher percentage than anyone else except the Episcopalians.

Episcopalian membership increased 16 percent between 1950 and 1955, and 16 percent again between 1955 and 1960. From 1960 to 1965, the increase slowed to 4.5 percent. Then the decline began. Beginning in 1965, Episcopalians have lost between 21.5 percent and 13 percent during each five-year period until the early 1990s.

The Presbyterian Church (USA) and its predecessor denominations fared about the same. The United Church of Christ has not lost members in double-digit terms during any five-year period, but its losses began even earlier than those of other denominations.[2]

More modest losses swept across all the other mainstream Protestant denominations. Table 1 below illustrates the dramatic change.

At the same time that mainstream Protestant denominations were losing members, the census figures showed the American population growing at the rate of approximately five percent every five years from 1965 to 1990. Bucking the decline were Roman Catholics and some conservative Protestant denominations.[3] Table 2 below demonstrates this pattern.

Mainstream Protestantism's loss of members since the 1960s obscures a longer trend. Since the late 1920s and early 1930s, these denominations have not grown as fast as the American population. As a result, mainstream Protestantism has been in *relative* decline for more than a half century, even though the *real* decline began in the 1960s.[4]

It must be acknowledged that it is notoriously difficult to compare church membership figures. Some denominations have relatively strict guidelines for maintaining these figures; other de-

Table 1. MAINSTREAM MEMBERSHIP DECLINE, 1947-1990*

Denomination	"Inclusive" Membership			Percent Change		
	1947	1965	1990	1947-1965	1965-1990	1947-1990
American Baptist Churches in the USA	1,592,349	1,559,103	1,535,971	-2.1%	-1.5%	-3.5%
Christian Church (Disciples of Christ)	1,889,066	1,918,471	1,039,692	+1.6%	-45.8%	-45.0%
Episcopal Church	2,155,514	3,429,153	2,446,050	+59.1%	-57.8%	+13.5%
Evangelical Lutheran Church in America	3,607,473	5,684,298	5,240,739	+57.6%	-7.8%	+45.3%
Presbyterian Church (USA)	2,969,382	4,254,460	2,847,437	+43.3%	-33.1%	-4.1%
Reformed Church in America	255,107	385,754	326,850	+34.0%	-15.0%	+22.0%
United Church of Christ	1,835,853	2,070,413	1,599,212	+12.8%	-22.8%	-12.9%
United Methodist Church	9,135,248	11,067,497	8,904,824	+21.2%	-19.5%	-2.5%

* These figures include membership in predecessor denominations where unions occurred. Constant H. Jacquet, Jr., ed., *Yearbook of American and Canadian Churches, 1990* (Nashville: Abingdon Press, 1990), supplemented by figures in the editions of the *Yearbook* for 1991 and 1992. For an analysis of the growth and decline among the Disciples of Christ, see D. Newell Williams, ed., *A Case Study of Mainstream Protestantism: The Disciples' Relation to American Culture, 1880-1980* (Grand Rapids, Mich.: Wm. B. Eerdmans Publishing Co., 1991), pp. 445-553.

Table 2. MEMBERSHIP GROWTH, 1965-1990*

Denomination	"Inclusive" Membership			Percent Change		
	1947	1965	1990	1947-1965	1965-1990	1947-1990
Assemblies of God	241,782	572,123	2,181,502	+137%	+281%	+802%
Church of God (Cleveland, Tennessee)	77,926	205,465	620,939	+164%	+202%	+697%
Church of God in Christ	300,000	413,000	5,499,875	+38%	+1231%	+1721%
Church of the Nazarene	201,487	343,380	561,296	+70%	+63%	+179%
Jehovah's Witnesses	N/A	330,358	825,570	N/A	+150%	N/A
Lutheran Church, Missouri Synod	1,422,513	2,692,889	2,602,849	+89%	-3.3%	+83%
Roman Catholic Church	24,402,124	46,246,175	58,568,015	+89%	+26%	+140%
Seventh Day Adventist Church	208,030	364,666	717,446	+75%	+97%	+245%
Southern Baptist Convention	6,079,305	10,770,573	15,038,409	+77%	+39%	+147%

* See note to Table 1 above.

nominations are much looser in their record keeping. Given these differences, caution should be exercised in comparisons of membership data.

Various theories have been used to explain the membership decline. Some argue the decline occurred because congregations tried to save money on assessments per member by aggressively removing inactive members from the roles. Others attribute it to poor leadership. A few insist that the church should be more relevant and therefore more active in social and political causes. But the most popular explanation has been that churches are too active and too political; they have driven their members into conservative churches.[5]

Research reveals that these theories are wrong, or at least inadequate, in accounting for the membership decline. Instead, researchers agree on two major conclusions. First, the changing demographics and changing family structures of the post-World War II era had a significant impact on mainstream Protestantism. Church membership grew during this era, in large measure, because of the high population of children comprising the baby boom generation. When the baby boom ended, membership soon declined. Second, mainstream Protestant churches generally do not lose their members to conservative churches. Instead, the vast majority of defectors do not affiliate with another church. Let us look at these explanations in greater detail.[6]

Demographics: Growth and Decline

The now famous baby boom started in 1946 and ended in 1964. Such a population explosion was both unprecedented and unexpected. The baby boomers have significantly affected American society and its institutions and will influence them well into the twenty-first century. One sociologist has compared the relation between the culture and the baby boom generation to a python swallowing a pig. At each stage of digestion, the snake is distorted.[7]

Wade Clark Roof and William McKinney's study, *American Mainline Religion,* along with other research, demonstrates how birth rates and family structure affect church membership. "Liberal

Protestants" had a birth rate of 2.27 children per family during the baby boom. After it ended, the rate declined to 1.60 children per family. In other words, even if "liberal Protestants" retained every child born into their membership today, the membership would still decline.[8]

The parents of the baby boom generation joined churches in part because they sought religious education for their children. One article which appeared in an academic journal used a biblical text to describe this pattern: "And a little child shall lead them."[9] Children brought their parents to church. When the baby boomers became adults, their parents sometimes left the church.

But most importantly, the baby boomers behaved very differently than their parents. They delayed marriage. When they married, they delayed having children, and they divorced at a much higher rate than their parents. When they had children, they had fewer than their parents.

The baby boom generation also pursued higher levels of education than previous generations. For example, 63 percent of Presbyterian baby boomers are college graduates. They are, moreover, geographically and occupationally mobile. Although baby boomers lived through the counter-cultural movements of the 1960s and 1970s, that experience did not leave much of an imprint on them aside from a distrust of institutions and strong individualism — traits they share with much of American society.[10]

The impact of the baby boomers on mainstream Protestant churches has been dramatic. Although they brought their parents to church, they have not affiliated with the church at the same rate as their parents did. Slightly less than half of the baby boomers are outside of the church. As a result, mainstream Protestant denominations are significantly older than the American population as a whole. As death claims more of their members, these denominations' failure to replace them with younger members spells difficulties in stabilizing membership at current levels and even greater difficulties for achieving growth.[11]

Wade Clark Roof has studied the religious behavior of the baby boomers in *A Generation of Seekers,* and Dean Hoge, Ben Johnson, and Donald Luidens focused on Presbyterian baby boomers in *Vanishing Boundaries.* The conclusions of these studies differ in nuances but agree about general patterns. The religious behavior of the baby boom generation can be charted in a bell-shaped curve. In the case of the Presbyterians, a small percentage have become fundamentalists, and a small percentage have lost all interest in religion. In between is the large bell of Presbyterian baby boomers, churched and unchurched, comprising 86 percent. The breakdown of the churched baby boomers is as follows:[12]

Active Presbyterians	29%
Other mainline Protestants	10%
Other churches (mainly Roman Catholic and Baptist)	7%
Fundamentalists	6%
TOTAL	**52%**

Therefore, about half of the baby boomers confirmed in the Presbyterian Church are still members of churches. Less than one-third remain Presbyterian. The rest are unchurched, but they are not a uniform group. Some attend church but do not belong to a congregation. Others are still members but do not attend. Some are uninvolved but retain religious beliefs. Here are the divisions among the unchurched baby boomers:[13]

Unchurched attenders	10%
Unchurched members	9%
Uninvolved but religious	21%
Unreligious	8%
TOTAL	**48%**

Roof's research on a broader sample of the baby boom generation came to similar conclusions. He grouped them as loyalists (33%), returnees (25%), and dropouts (42%).[14]

Some baby boomers are returning to church as they eventually marry and have children. In fact, the desire for religious education for their children is a powerful motivation for church affiliation, just as it was for their parents.[15]

But changes in family structure have also had a powerful influence on church membership. Since 1970, there has been a 100 percent increase in the number of single parent households, from 4 million to 8 million homes. The number of mothers working outside the home increased 65 percent, from 10.2 million in 1970 to 16.8 million in 1990. Married couples with children now make up only 26 percent of the American population, compared with 40 percent in 1970.[16]

The Presbyterian baby boomer study revealed how marriage status and family structures dramatically affect church affiliation. Among Presbyterians, 79 percent of the members, 84 percent of the elders, and 90 percent of the pastors are married, and 80 percent of each category has children. The unchurched Presbyterian baby boomers, however, are much more likely to be single, divorced, or married for a second time, and less likely to have children.[17]

Furthermore, the increase in the number of both spouses working outside the home has escalated the pressure of time. Church membership and participation frequently suffer. As a pastor observed about baby boomers in a Chicago congregation: "Their mantra is: 'I'm busy.'"

The growing diversity of the American population since World War II has also complicated the prospects for growth in mainstream Protestant denominations. In 1950, 11 percent of the American population was non-white, and 82 percent of the non-whites were African Americans. The Immigration Act of 1965 opened the United States to more immigrants from Latin America, Asia, and Africa. By 1990, 20 percent of the population was non-white: 12 percent African American, 3 percent Asian, 1 percent American Indian, and 4 percent other races. By 1990, the Census Bureau had begun counting people of Hispanic origin, who come from a variety of racial groups. In 1990, they comprised 9 percent of the total population. Accelerating this growth are higher birth rates among non-whites and Hispanics than the birth rate of the white population.[18]

American mainstream Protestant denominations have drawn their members largely from the white population. Their members are not reproducing themselves fast enough to stem the membership loss, and population growth is more rapid in the non-white population of the United States.

Choice: The Phenomenon of Switching

Research on membership decline also demonstrates the importance of switching denominations. Americans have always been religiously mobile, especially as their educational and economic status changed. A once common joke holds that a Methodist is a Baptist who finished high school; a Presbyterian is a Methodist who finished college; and an Episcopalian is a Presbyterian who joined the country club. Such a description is exaggerated, but it had some factual basis in the past. Increasingly, however, that kind of description is not true. The educational and economic status of members is now less likely to play a significant role in church affiliation and religious mobility.

Switching is rampant in American religion, especially among baby boomers, and its power is growing among all American religious groups. Denominational loyalties are weak. Switching is common even among Roman Catholics, despite the fact that the Catholic Church formerly retained its members and its young at very high rates.[19]

The willingness to change denominations is higher among mainstream Protestant denominations and lower among conservative churches. On the one hand, many who believe that mainstream Protestants have defected to conservative churches are surprised to learn that mainstream denominations receive more conservative members than they lose to conservative churches. On the other hand, more people defect from mainstream Protestant churches to non-affiliation than do members from conservative denominations. The net loss is greater for mainstream churches.

Roof and McKinney tested the quality as well as the quantity of the "switchers." Those who transferred their membership into conservative denominations were about as loyal as they had been in the mainstream denominations. They found that those switching to the "right" were also as regular in attendance and as financially supportive as those born and reared in conservative churches.[20]

The more numerous switchers from conservative to mainstream churches were also about as loyal in activities and stewardship as lifelong members of the denomination. But compared to conservative congregations, few of the mainstream churches invited or demanded very high levels of participation from their traditional or new members.[21]

Roof and McKinney point to a "new voluntarism" among mainstream Protestants, who now choose religious involvement or lack of it based on whether they find self-fulfillment in belonging to a church. Almost gone is any sense of one particular Christian body being "right" while the others are "wrong." Denominational loyalties are weaker. Instead, people speak of the "wholeness and experience in faith." People seek to discover themselves, often outside of institutions; religion has become local and private among the vast majority of Americans.[22]

People still say they pray, believe firmly in God, and seek to live "moral" lives. But according to a Gallup poll, 81 percent of churched people agreed with the statement, "One should arrive at his or her own religious beliefs independent of a church or synagogue." The percentage agreeing with the statement among the unchurched is only slightly higher (86%).[23]

Roof argues that even though the baby boomers are especially prone to switching and leaving the church entirely, this does not mean they have abandoned religion. Instead, they contrast what it means to be "religious" (which they associate with churches) with what it means to be "spiritual" (which they associate with God). The baby boomers are, says Roof, "a generation of seekers," searching for the spiritual more often than the religious.[24]

Chain bookstores may have recognized and capitalized on this phenomenon long before the churches. For evidence, one need only peruse their shelves in the religion section. Most bookshops have at least a modest selection of books and tapes under a sign marked "Religion." But increasingly one discovers another expanding section often labeled "New Age," which includes materials ranging from the latest CD of nature sounds to information on channeling and the modern or refashioned wica (witchcraft) movement.

The conclusions are clear. Sociological factors have played a major if not dominant role in mainstream Protestant membership decline. Demographics — changes in birth rates, family structures, and immigration — and freedom of religious choice have radically changed the culture in which these churches minister. The mainstream Protestant churches have been affected negatively by these changes. At the same time, these new realities can clarify and focus the opportunities for outreach in the future.

Sociological factors, however, do not tell the entire story of the decline in mainstream Protestant membership. These denominations also unwittingly adopted programs and policies that contributed to the downturn in membership.

The Debate over Denominational Priorities

Before World War II, the priorities of mainstream Protestant denominations were fairly obvious: domestic and international mission, evangelism and church extension, Christian education and publication. These priorities continued into the 1950s, and all of the mainstream Protestant denominations launched major evangelism campaigns and aggressive new church development programs.

Presbyterians called their efforts the New Life Movement or the United Evangelistic Crusade or the Presbyterian Program of Progress. For Methodists, the United Evangelistic Mission was the banner of evangelism in the fifties. American Baptists emphasized lay participation and local church involvement in reaching the unchurched. Congregationalists coordinated their program through the Commission on Evangelism and Devotional Life. Episcopalians promoted Parish Life Weekends, designed to nurture the faith of members gathered in small groups. In the Reformed Church in America, the evangelism program was "Preaching, Teaching, Reaching," and it included weekend visits by evangelism teams.

These evangelistic efforts were reinforced by the favorable climate for religion in the 1950s. The press described "a return to religion," and churches clearly benefited from a cultural mood that encouraged religious belief and affiliation. In the post–World War II age of the "organization man," conformity and respectability were highly valued and often associated with church membership.

Mainstream Protestant church leaders were often somewhat skeptical about the depth and quality of the religious revival of the fifties. Some sharply criticized the newly popular Billy Graham for his preaching, revivalistic techniques, and theology.[25]

Gradually emerging was a critique of evangelism focused on the individual and individual salvation. Instead, mainstream Protestant leaders emphasized a salvation for the service of others, and an evangelism as the pursuit of social justice. These changing accents were sounded with special urgency during the 1960s and 1970s as mainstream Protestants became more conscious of the crises of American society spawned by the crises of race, poverty, and the cities.[26]

The denominations responded by broadening mission programs and putting money behind their ethical concerns. In some denominations, such as the Presbyterians and the United Church of Christ, evangelism virtually disappeared as a denominational concern at the national level. For other denominations, such as the Methodists, evangelism programs faced stiff competition from other denominational causes. The result was sharply reduced financial support. Even into the 1960s, the Methodist Board of Evangelism had a staff of almost fifty professionals. After a merger and restructuring in the late sixties and early seventies, the Board of Evangelism was renamed the Section on Evangelism of the General Board of Discipleship. The staff was pruned to eight professionals, and its budget became emaciated by inflation and competition from other priorities. From 1975 to 1986, the Section on Evangelism's budget increased only 8 percent, while inflation rose 123 percent.[27]

The rise and fall of evangelism programs in mainstream Protestant churches has a complementary chapter: new church development. The Great Depression, World War II, and wartime construction quotas dampened new church development until the late 1940s. Pent-up demand, plus the growth of suburbs, made the 1950s a golden era of new churches. All the mainstream Protestant denominations made a major commitment to starting new congregations in the post-war era.

In the 1960s and 1970s, priorities shifted away from new church development toward other causes. Only after the severity of membership decline impressed itself upon denominational leaders in the 1980s did new church development begin to increase again — but not at the rates of the 1950s.

The growth and decline pattern of new church development is common to all of the mainstream Protestant churches. The

American Baptist Churches founded 389 new churches in the 1950s, 254 in the 1960s, 168 in the 1970s, and 402 in the 1980s. United Methodists launched an average of 124 new congregations each year from 1958 to 1961 alone. By 1966–69, the average had plummeted to 49, and from 1970 to 1974 the average was only 20. Then there was a modest revival of Methodist new church development, and by the eighties they averaged approximately 60 new churches each year.[28]

One example from the Presbyterians is especially instructive. Charlotte, North Carolina had one of the largest concentrations of Presbyterians in the nation. From 1946 to 1966, the local presbytery averaged one new church start every year. From 1967 to 1979, no new Presbyterian congregations were begun. Yet during the 1970s Charlotte grew dramatically and became a major urban center of the South.[29]

On the positive side, when mainstream Protestants reentered the field of new church development in the eighties, they recognized the importance of reaching out to new constituencies. From 1966 to 1969, only 7 percent of new United Methodist congregations were racial-ethnic minority churches. But in the period 1980–84, 43 percent were formed with Asian, Hispanic, African American, and Native American Methodists. Similar strategies were employed by other mainstream Protestant denominations, with varying degrees of commitment and success.[30]

The debate over denominational priorities was fueled by an internal critique of the church and its mission. From the academy as well as the pulpit came a call for mainstream Protestants to reassess their relationship to the values and institutions of American culture. Mainstream Protestants were told to confront and confess their complicity in racism, poverty, and war. The imperatives of the gospel were compared to the priorities of the church, and the church was found wanting.

At the same time, the church growth movement, led by Donald McGavran and others, began to mobilize energy and funding among evangelicals within and outside of mainstream Protestant denominations. Because of its emphasis on "the homogenous unit principle" (congregations thrive when they consist of people of similar social backgrounds), the church growth movement seemed to represent what mainstream Protestant critics wanted to purge from the church — racism and class bias.[31]

The salvation of the individual and the transformation of society, evangelism in words and evangelism in deeds — these creative tensions in Christianity were polarized in mainstream Protestantism during the 1960s. As early as 1968, when membership decline had only begun, the United Presbyterian Church's Board of National Missions declared that "the Church has no warrant for substituting a statistical graph for a cross." Invoking what would become a common biblical theme for fending off concern about membership loss, the board continued, "If [the church] takes seriously the gospel of its Lord; if it is willing to lose its life that it may find it, the apparent winnowing of its membership may yet prove to be its restoring."[32]

These powerful words indirectly expressed the need and desire to cope with that tumultuous year — 1968. During that year occurred the assassinations of Martin Luther King, Jr., and Robert F. Kennedy, urban riots, and a heightened concern about the escalation of the war in Vietnam. Few mainstream Protestants today would fault the church for believing that redefining its moral passion or redirecting its financial resources was necessary. Ironically, what was initiated with the best of intentions and the highest of ideals was to have unseen consequences.

The internal critique of the church contributed to the fragmented understanding of mission and evangelism in mainstream Protestantism. The temper of the times since the 1960s has not been conducive to seeing the contending mission priorities of verbal and physical witness as complementary, rather than competitive, or to advocating the importance of programs that sustain churches as institutions.

Furthermore, the growth of new church development during the fifties, modest decline in the sixties, substantial reductions in the seventies, and partial recovery in the eighties has tragically coincided with the changing demographics of American society. Researchers have discovered that the majority of denominational growth comes from starting new churches, not from the growth of existing congregations.[33] Just as the baby boom ended and the demographics supporting membership growth changed, mainstream Protestants reduced their commitment to at least one program that offered them some hope of resisting decline.

Congregations: Possibilities for Growth

By the 1990s, mainstream Protestants have adjusted again. Some seminaries have added faculty positions in evangelism. Conferences on evangelism have multiplied. Seizing the initiative, congregations and regional governing bodies have founded new churches and redeveloped others, including congregations drawn from racial-ethnic minority groups. The much derided church growth movement has won cautious and critical approval among many mainstream Protestant denominations, at least for its emphasis on outreach.

But people are increasingly asking important questions: Why do some churches decline while others grow? Why do some people join churches while others leave or never join?

Gradually both church leaders and researchers have come to a startlingly simple but intriguing conclusion about church growth and decline: *People join or leave congregations, not denominations.* In other words, demographics, national trends, and denominational policies are important in describing why *denominations* decline or grow. But these factors do not fully explain why *congregations* decline or grow or why people choose or reject church membership.

While the answers to the above questions are simple, they are also extraordinarily complex. Most importantly, these answers are extremely helpful in understanding how mainstream Protestants can address three decades of membership loss.

The factors that contribute to congregational decline are fairly obvious. Demographics again play a significant role. A church in central Nebraska where the population is declining is unlikely to grow. Likewise, hundreds of mainstream Protestant urban congregations have declined because of the "white flight" to the suburbs. Location is another important variable. One Presbyterian church in the Louisville area did not have a viable congregation because it had no parking. After it moved to a new location less than a mile away, people started to attend and join.[34]

Conflict is a major factor in congregational decline. Interestingly, people rarely leave congregations because of national controversies such as civil rights, war, and abortion. Instead, they usually defect over local and very particular issues — the pastor did not visit someone in the hospital; the order of worship was changed; someone insulted a parishioner's child. The list is endless, but the point is crucial: local conflict rather than national controversy causes most loss of members from congregations.[35]

People also leave congregations because they find no help in a time of crisis, grow alienated from the minister or members, move to another place, experience a life passage, or simply find that attending and participating are unfulfilling. Interviews with those who leave reveal that they are rarely angry with Christianity or the church; rather, the alienated are apathetic.[36]

Growing congregations exhibit important differences. Usually, but not always, growing congregations benefit from favorable demographics and location. More important, however, are several significant characteristics identified by researchers:

1. *Growing congregations want to grow.* This is perhaps the simplest but most difficult hurdle for most congregations to leap. The decision to grow means the decision to endure the disruption of including new and different people, the acceptance of new leadership, and the development of new programs.[37] Despite a verbally expressed desire to grow, many congregations contradict their aspiration with their behavior. For example, the annual report of one congregation we visited announced proudly that evangelism was its number one priority. At the end of the report, the budget revealed that one hundred dollars had been allocated for evangelism.

Congregations can be misled to believe that numerical growth is the only, indeed the preferred, goal of Christian discipleship. Numerical growth may be unlikely for some congregations. But congregations can also grow in other ways, as Loren Mead has suggested. They can focus on deepening the maturity of their members' faith, strengthening the vitality of their life as a community, and expanding their mission in their communities and throughout the world.[38]

Being committed to growth is the key, rather than preserving the insulation and isolation of the congregation.

2. Growing congregations are outwardly oriented and highly involved in outreach and service. Contrary to some assumptions that growing churches are introspective, these congregations are remarkably active in reaching out to others beyond the congregation. Their members believe the church has something to say and offer. Therefore, they invite people to church; they accept visitors and new members warmly; they orient their worship style so that it is more seeker-friendly; and they volunteer for service projects and for responsibilities within the congregation.[39]

3. Growing congregations have effective leaders and a compelling message. What constitutes effective leadership is one of the most debated and convoluted issues in American churches today, not to speak of American society. Nevertheless, like the judge who declared that he could not define pornography but that he knew it when he saw it, effective leadership is obvious when it is present. It makes an enormous difference in congregational life, and is an important key to understanding why some congregations grow and others decline.[40]

Leadership obviously refers to the ministers who lead congregations. Pastors or priests of growing congregations are generally good preachers, compassionate in pastoral care, well organized, and able to relate to people. Behind all of these characteristics is that intangible quality called spirituality — being able to represent and present the gospel of Jesus Christ.

But an equally important ingredient in effective leadership is the quality of leadership among members themselves — people who have a strong commitment to the Christian faith, who see the church as essential to the well-being of individuals and society, and who are willing to invest their time and resources to make the church vital and faithful.

Studies of growing congregations conclude with a paradox: leaders produce vital congregations; but vital congregations produce leaders. Neither exists without the other. *What makes these congregations vital is their spiritual depth — a compelling and persuasive communication of the gospel.*

One illustration helps point out how these ingredients — willingness to grow, outward orientation, leadership, and Christian commitment — contribute to a growing congregation. In Guston,

Kentucky, there is a Presbyterian church that was founded in the 1890s. Guston is so small that there is no stoplight, and the Presbyterian church is not even located on Main Street. Until the 1980s, the Guston church had part-time pastors — usually seminary students or retired ministers.

Then a middle-aged minister, recently retired from the army and just out of seminary, accepted a call to the Guston church. His army pension enabled him to accept the minuscule salary the church could offer. When he arrived, the membership had dwindled to thirteen. He began a tireless effort to get to know and be known by people in the area. He invited them to church, assuring them that they did not have to give money — which apparently had been a large stumbling block for many.

Every Sunday he found some way of affirming people who came. He gave out ribbons to the choir; he publicly celebrated birthdays and anniversaries; he mourned the death of family members and friends; he rejoiced in births and marriages. One Sunday a woman in her eighties was baptized and became a member. She had attended the church for decades. When the pastor inquired why she had waited so long to join the church, she replied, "You're the first one who asked me."

After four years, the membership had grown to more than one hundred. For the first time in nearly a century, the congregation supported a full-time pastor at the minimum salary recommended by the presbytery. The congregation celebrated having "our own pastor."

Why, then, do people join congregations?

1. People are invited. An invitation from a friend or family member is the primary reason cited by members for choosing a particular congregation. Certainly the style, content, and quality of the congregation's worship and program are crucial ingredients choosing to affiliate with a congregation. But in a majority of cases, someone bringing another to that church is the most important factor.[41]

2. People choose to join. As noted before, choice is a powerful factor shaping the life of churches in contemporary America. But choice operates more freely and creates more challenges for churches in a society that no longer reinforces or supports religious behavior and belief. Some researchers urge congregations to adopt "marketing" strategies to attract and retain members.[42]

Many find such strategies repugnant; they reject the idea of the church as an institution "selling" a particular "product." At the same time, it is clear that contemporary churches are more than ever before buffeted by the powerful influence of choice. Family, educational and economic status, and denominational allegiance no longer strongly influence — as they once did — individuals's decisions to join congregations. Instead, people choose.[43]

3. When people choose congregations, they are seeking fulfillment in programs that meet their "needs." The baby boomers are the most individualistic and consumer-minded group in American society, and mainstream Protestant baby boomers are insistent that their needs be addressed. This poses an inevitable predicament, often phrased in this way: Does a church offer what prospective members want or what the church thinks they need?

Such a question, however, is misleading. It assumes that what potential members want and what the church thinks they need are quite far apart. Are they really? Research on the baby boomers indicates that these seekers are certainly demanding new forms of congregational life. But they are attracted to these forms because of an age-old search, one in which the church has long found its purpose — the search for meaning.

Most of the research considered thus far has emphasized that sociological, not theological, factors are crucial in determining church affiliation. But recent research indicates that the baby boomers do not reject Christianity itself as meaningless. Many find the Christianity presented by mainstream Protestant congregations to be thin gruel for infusing meaning into their lives. According to one researcher, one member from a mainstream Protestant church finally left because "there was no meat; I got fed a lot of Twinkies."[44]

Sociologists Hoge, Johnson, and Luidens have concluded that belief is the most powerful indicator of an individual baby boomer's decision to join or leave the church. What people "need" is what the church can offer: a sense of meaning in life through belonging to God.[45]

Thus the challenge before mainstream Protestantism is this:

Will the church be flexible enough to interpret the gospel message in appropriately new forms to fit the demands and needs of our changing times? At the same time, will its proclamation of the Christian gospel be faithful to the church's traditions and sufficiently substantive to provide purpose for those who struggle to make sense of their lives?

3. The Predicament of Pluralism: Mainstream Protestant Theology in the Twentieth Century

IN 1835, Alexander Campbell, one of the leaders of the movement that became the Disciples of Christ, proclaimed: "One God, one moral system, one Bible. If nature be a system, religion is no less so. . . . The Bible is to the intellectual and moral world of man what the sun is to the planets in our system — the fountain and source of light and life, spiritual and eternal." He continued, "The Bible is a book of facts, not of opinions, theories, abstract generalities, nor of verbal definitions. These facts reveal God and man, and contain within them the reasons for all piety and righteousness, or what is commonly called religion and morality." The Bible, Campbell concluded, was "the constitution" of the world.[1]

Despite the dizzying proliferation of denominations and sects in the early nineteenth century, few American Protestants would have disputed Campbell's view of "one God, one moral system, one Bible."

By the late twentieth century, everything had changed. Writing in the mid-1970s, pollster Daniel Yankelovich described the transformation of beliefs and values: "Where strict norms had prevailed in the fifties and sixties, now all was pluralism and freedom of choice: to marry or live together; to have children early or postpone them, perhaps forever; to come out of the closet or stay in; to keep the old job or return to school; to make commitments or hang loose; to change careers, spouses, houses, states of residence, states of mind."[2]

The change, of course, did not come as suddenly as
Yankelovich suggested. Pluralism and freedom of choice have been
embedded in American culture for centuries, and even in Alexander
Campbell's day there was considerable religious diversity. But beliefs
and values have shifted, especially since the late nineteenth century.
Mainstream Protestants in particular have sought to understand,
influence, and tolerate the growing complexity of the modern
world. At the end of the twentieth century, few saw reality in terms
of "one God, one moral system, one Bible." Instead, as they
looked at their world, they viewed diversity of religions, pluralism
of values, and various scriptural authorities.

From one perspective, this is a story about the growth of
American cultural pluralism — the broadening participation of different peoples and the acceptance and toleration of divergent values
and ways of life. From another perspective, this is a saga about a
group of Protestant churches struggling to widen and deepen the
scope of the church's beliefs and practice.

In both the culture and the church, this pluralism is a predicament. It places in conflict two positive values: the toleration of
diversity and the assertion of truth. How mainstream Protestants
responded to the challenges of pluralism is a powerful illustration
of both their problems and their promise in the late twentieth
century.

The Critical Period

The critical period for the influential Protestant denominations of
the nineteenth century began approximately with the Civil War and
extended into the 1920s and 1930s. When Paul Carter wrote a
history of religion in late nineteenth-century America, he called it
The Spiritual Crisis of the Gilded Age and began the book with the
memorable words from Dickens's *Tale of Two Cities:* "It was the
best of times, it was the worst of times."[3]

On the one hand, it seemed, Protestantism had never enjoyed
more prominence in American society. During the 1890s, New
York newspapers devoted at least an entire page each Monday to
reports of sermons in the Protestant pulpits of the city. In 1875

when America's most prominent preacher, Henry Ward Beecher, was on trial for sexual misconduct, his stature was so great that the press covered the proceedings in extensive detail. The formation of the Evangelical Alliance in the United States in 1867 symbolically demonstrated both the unity and the power of late nineteenth-century Protestantism. By the end of the century, Americans dominated Protestant world missions, and the mainstream Protestants led the way. The Edinburgh World Missionary Conference in 1910 attracted 1,200 representatives from across the globe; the seven major American Protestant denominations sent anywhere from 20 to 123 representatives each. American Methodists alone sponsored more than 10 percent of those who attended.[4]

A perceptive English observer, Lord Bryce, concluded in 1888, "The matter may be summed up by saying that Christianity is in fact understood to be, though not the legally established religion, yet the national religion." He continued, "So far from thinking their commonwealth godless, the Americans conceive that the religious character of a government consists in nothing but the religious belief of the individual citizens, and the conformity of their conduct to that belief. They deem the general acceptance of Christianity to be one of the main sources of their national prosperity, and their nation a special object of Divine Favour."[5]

A Christian nation — forged not by law, but by belief and behavior: for most in late nineteenth-century America, this was a powerful image of national identity. Many Episcopalians, Presbyterians, and Methodists of the era were comfortable. A steadily deflationary economy meant that money acquired more value rather than less. God had indeed blessed America.

On the other hand, the prosperity of the U.S. disguised a bleaker side of American society: the increasing segregation of black Americans in the South, the seizure of Native American territories, the secondary status of women, and the growing gap between rich and poor.

What was obvious at the time were the monumental changes affecting America, especially its cities. Immigration recovered slowly after the Civil War; during the decade from 1860 to 1870, approximately 2 million people migrated to the United States. Soon the migration turned into a tidal wave; in only a few years from 1881 to 1884, 2.5 million immigrants came into this country. During the 1880s alone, 5,247,000 people entered the U.S. The arrivals were not only new Americans, but "new immigrants" who were fleeing southern and eastern Europe and Asia. Most did not speak English. The majority were not Protestant; they were Roman Catholic, Eastern Orthodox, Jewish, or practitioners of one of the Eastern religions. Along with southern blacks, they settled in cities, especially in the North, and these urban areas grew at astronomical rates during the late nineteenth century.[6]

The immigrants and new urban dwellers became the work force for the emerging American industrial colossus. Before the Civil War, the United States was last in coal, iron, and steel production compared to France, Germany, and Great Britain. By 1900, the United States was producing more iron, coal, and steel than France and Germany combined, and much more than Great Britain.[7]

As American society became an urbanized, industrial society with a much more diverse population, American Protestants experienced new and troubling challenges to their beliefs and values. Charles Darwin's *Origin of Species* attracted little notice in 1859 when it first appeared, but after the Civil War the impact of evolutionary science undermined the Christian confidence in the biblical account of creation. "Higher" biblical criticism revealed that there were even two accounts of creation in Genesis, and this scholarship probed the historical accuracy of biblical narratives. The new social sciences of psychology and sociology explored human personality and the structures of society that shaped values and behavior. The numerous American missionaries abroad heightened American Protestant's awareness of the power and appeal of other world religions.[8]

In both pulpits and pews, new questions and new doubts appeared. At stake was the authority and truth of Christianity, especially the evangelical Protestantism of nineteenth-century America. It was a new world of pluralism — with various truths, diverse values, and different cultures.

Most thoughtful Protestants were at least troubled, but some sailed through the storm with serene conviction that Christianity had lost none of its authority. For instance, Woodrow Wilson reflected on the religious confusion of his age and declared in 1889:

"I used to wonder vaguely why I did not have the same deep-reaching spiritual difficulties that I read of other young men having. I *saw* the intellectual difficulties but I was not *troubled* by them: they seem to have no connection with my faith in the essentials of the religion I had been taught. Unorthodox in my reading of the standards of the faith, I am nevertheless orthodox in my faith. I am capable, it would seem, of being satisfied spiritually without being satisfied intellectually."[9]

While it is impossible to capture the complex variety of the Protestant response to modern America, three types of reactions predominated. One option emphasized protest and resistance. Perhaps the best term for describing this movement is conservative Protestantism. The label is ambiguous and can refer to evangelicals, fundamentalists, pentecostals, and charismatics, even though there are significant differences among them. For example, many evangelicals who emphasize the importance of conversion and biblical authority resist being labeled as fundamentalist. Many streams of fundamentalism in turn reject what they consider to be the extreme emphasis on the doctrine of the Holy Spirit and speaking in tongues in pentecostalism.[10] Nevertheless, each of these groups can be labeled conservative Protestant, and this term can even be applied to a significant portion of mainstream Protestants in the late twentieth century.

The conservatives distrusted "higher" criticism of the Bible and affirmed the Bible as infallible (completely trustworthy in its teachings and doctrine) or inerrant (without significant textual or historical error). Christian doctrines did not need to be adjusted to the modern world. Instead, people needed to grasp the wisdom and truth of unchanging Christian beliefs. History was the record of the growth of human sin; as human welfare deteriorated, Jesus Christ would come again to judge the world and redeem the righteous.[11]

A second option was accommodation and adjustment. According to historian William Hutchison, this is "the modernist impulse" in American Protestantism.[12] Eventually known as "liberal Protestants," the advocates of modernism accepted the higher criticism of the Bible. They argued that Christian doctrines must be reinterpreted to make sense to the modern mind. They also proclaimed

that history, like nature, was evolutionary — it was the gradual
unfolding of God's benevolent design for the world. History was
the story of progress, and liberal Protestants sought to adapt the
Christian faith to the social and intellectual transformation of the
late nineteenth and early twentieth century. The modernists confi-
dently believed in God's providence, as well as their own crucial
role in making sure that God's will was done, on earth if not in
heaven. Some of them argued that the church needed something
new — "a social gospel" to address the political, social, and
economic realities of American society.[13]

In between these two religious options stood the majority of
mainstream Protestants. They sought to reinterpret and adapt the
Christian gospel to a changing world. Always leaning more in the
direction of the modernists than the conservatives, this group of
centrist Protestants accepted the Scriptures as carrying special authority, but they employed the insights of biblical criticism and
refused to designate their Bible as inerrant. They sought to retran-
slate Christian belief into a new vernacular much as the modernists
did. These Protestants, however, were less willing than the modernists to accommodate so completely to modern science. They
were also far less optimistic about the inevitable progress of sinful
humanity.

The contest between conservatives and modernists, as well as
the quandary of those in the middle, came into sharp focus in the
Presbyterian fundamentalist controversy during the 1920s. Modernism had very few advocates in American Presbyterianism of that
day. But some moderate leaders did object to the strictness and
rigidity with which the doctrinal standards of the faith were en-
forced. Their opponents, the fundamentalists, insisted on doctrinal
precision to preserve the purity of the church. The five classic
"fundamentals" were:

1. The inerrancy of Scripture;
2. The virgin birth of Jesus;
3. The bodily resurrection of Jesus;
4. The historical accuracy of Jesus' miracles;
5. The substitutionary atonement (to cancel God's judgment of
   human sin, Jesus died as a substitute for humanity).

Premillennialism — the belief that Christ would return to earth before the millennium (Christ's thousand-year reign) would begin — also eventually became associated with most forms of twentieth-century fundamentalism.[14]

Two characteristics of American fundamentalism are crucial, for they shaped the movement throughout the twentieth century, as well as across denominations. First, fundamentalists sought to define the irreducible core of Christian belief. Second, fundamentalists sought to define those doctrines as precisely as possible. For example, even though there have been many ways of understanding the atonement throughout Christian history, fundamentalists insisted on the substitutionary theory of atonement as the only acceptable alternative.

Well-defined boundaries versus flexible boundaries, enforcement of precise understanding versus toleration of various interpretations — these tensions mark the history of many Protestant denominations in the twentieth century, especially the mainstream Protestant churches. The evangelical consensus of the nineteenth century was fractured by contending forces. Each group rightly claimed to be heirs of their evangelical predecessors. In the aftermath of the Civil War, another civil war erupted within American Protestantism, and it has shaped the history of the churches and molded the piety of millions in the twentieth century.[15]

The Re-Forming Period

The period of the re-forming of American Protestantism begins symbolically in 1933. That year marks the repeal of Prohibition. The passage of the Eighteenth Amendment was perhaps the greatest legislative victory in the Protestant attempt to create a Christian America. The demise of prohibition was a sign of Protestantism's disestablishment — the end of its domination of American culture. The 1930s also represent Western culture in crisis — a global economic depression, the rise of fascism in Europe, and the threat of communism.[16]

A powerful theological movement, "neo-orthodoxy," emerged during the 1930s, addressing not only the theological battles of the early twentieth century but also the crisis of the West. As a movement, it had little unity; its representatives often rejected the title "neo-orthodox" and criticized other members of the school. Because of its urgency about the unravelling of both church and society, this "new" orthodoxy was sometimes called the "theology of crisis." Since it tried to recover central doctrines of the Reformation, it was also described as "neo-Reformation" theology.[17] Its best-known proponents were Karl Barth, Emil Brunner, Reinhold Niebuhr, and H. Richard Niebuhr.

As a theological strategy, neo-orthodoxy sought a middle ground between conservatism and liberalism. Neo-orthodoxy recognized the importance of biblical criticism but retained a strong emphasis on biblical authority. It was sharply critical of the conservative tendency to define the Christian life in terms of rigid moralisms — e.g., prohibition of drinking, dancing, card playing, etc. It also protested against forms of pietism that excluded political and social concerns from the Christian faith.[18]

The neo-orthodox objection to liberalism was equally pointed. The fatal flaws in liberalism, the neo-orthodox theologians declared, were its naive optimism about human nature and its willingness to identify the Christian faith with contemporary culture. In their desire to adapt Christianity to the modern world, liberals watered down Christianity and abandoned its distinctive affirmations. H. Richard Niebuhr summarized the neo-orthodox indictment of liberalism in one sentence. In liberal theology, "A God without wrath brought men without sin into a kingdom without judgment through the ministrations of Christ without a cross."[19]

In trying to forge a middle ground between conservatism and liberalism, neo-orthodoxy represents the theological spirit of mainstream Protestantism in the twentieth century. In 1944, Princeton Seminary president John A. Mackay launched the journal *Theology Today*. His lead editorial was a call for renewal through recovery of the church's theological heritage, and a summons to the church to reform the world. "Why . . . should they only appear to possess conviction and authority who belong to an extremist fringe on the religious right or left?" Mackay asked. "Why does not the center become articulate, and move forward with clear eye and passionate heart?" The answer, he declared, was "because those at the center have in these last times largely ceased to understand the faith to which they are heirs, and have come to wear as a conventional badge what they should unfurl as a crusading banner." The desired goal, he maintained, was a theological stance that rejected both "a fantastic apocalypticism . . . that despairs of this world" and "a utopian humanism that deifies it."[20]

Neo-orthodoxy drew from a variety of Christian traditions and schools of philosophy, but its proponents sounded common themes. The Bible is authoritative for Christian faith and life through the work of the Holy Spirit, but it is not inerrant. Theology, confessions, and doctrine are central to the Christian faith, but they are human and therefore imperfect attempts to describe a divine mystery. Sin is a condition of human nature, not simply wrong or misguided behavior. Sin is characteristic not only of individuals but also of institutions and society itself. Even though sin infects all of human culture, Christians should not shun social and political involvement but rather work toward society's redemption through Jesus Christ. The neo-orthodox impulse to declare first "on the one hand" and then "on the other hand" resulted in another descriptive label: "dialectical theology," or theology in dialogue with the world and with other theological points of view. It was a theology that mediated between extremes, as well as between various Christian traditions.[21]

By the 1940s and 1950s, neo-orthodoxy became the dominant theological perspective among mainstream Protestant leaders. A "biblical theology" movement in biblical studies emphasized many of the same perspectives. Neo-orthodox themes strongly influenced a renewal of Protestant worship through a recovery of the richness of earlier liturgical practice in Christianity. Its theologians were the preeminent leaders of the ecumenical movement of the mid-twentieth century. After World War II, they shaped the work of the National Council of Churches and the World Council of Churches. The height of neo-orthodoxy's influence coincided with the religious revival of the 1950s, even though many criticized the revival as shallow and superficial. Together with biblical theology and ecumenism, neo-orthodoxy triumphed in mainstream Protestant theological seminaries, in the major doctoral programs in theology, in religious studies departments in colleges and universities, and in the sermons and Sunday School materials of mainstream Protestant churches.[22]

As neo-orthodoxy enjoyed both cultural and religious prominence, however, conservative Protestantism was mobilizing and gaining strength. Beginning in the late nineteenth and early twentieth centuries, conservative Protestants began creating a counter-culture of alternative institutions and associations to compete with mainstream Protestant denominations. Instead of colleges and universities, they founded Bible institutes and Bible colleges. Rather than supporting missionary work through denominations, they launched "faith missions" (missionaries supported by individuals or congregations) and new independent missionary societies. They also began to form and support para-church groups, especially for youth, a trend which has continued throughout the twentieth century. Through these efforts, conservative Protestants attempted to maintain their conservative faith against the influence of mainstream Protestantism and liberalism.[23]

After World War II, conservative Protestants shifted and broadened their strategy. One wing, "neo-evangelicalism," took tentative steps toward mainstream Protestantism and neo-orthodoxy by emphasizing Christian social responsibility and by cautiously accepting some forms of biblical criticism. Conservatives also sought a more prominent voice in American Protestantism, and three developments symbolize the new offensive they launched to acquire greater religious and cultural influence. In 1943, the conservatives founded their own ecumenical forum, the National Association of Evangelicals, as an alternative to the Federal or National Council of Churches. In 1947 they started Fuller Theological Seminary, intentionally modeled after the Princeton Theological Seminary of the early twentieth century. In 1956, Billy Graham and others started *Christianity Today* as an alternative to *The Christian Century*.[24]

The neo-orthodox movement remained deeply distrustful of conservative Protestantism and its fundamentalist orientation. Neo-orthodox theologians were also uncomfortable with the evangelical Protestant heritage that they shared with conservative Protestants. The civil war continued through the 1950s, each party staking out familiar ground.

Two issues in particular functioned as the litmus test between conservative and liberal Protestants — the doctrine of Scripture and the church's social and political role. Conservatives continued to insist on the inerrancy and/or infallibility of Scripture, while liberals redefined Scripture's authority by recognizing it as the Word of God only when interpreted through the Holy Spirit. Conservatives remained uneasy with an active political role for the church — either through political pronouncements or through social action — while liberals insisted that the gospel must address critical issues in the world. Partly as a result of such insistence, mainstream Protestant seminaries expanded significantly their teaching of social ethics.[25]

A central theme in neo-orthodoxy was its criticism of American society, as well as of the church as an institution. Nineteenth-century evangelicalism, neo-orthodox theologians said, too quickly baptized the values and institutions of American society as Christian. Beginning with the social gospel of the late nineteenth and early twentieth century, distinctions were drawn between what is Christian and what is American. Neo-orthodoxy continued and deepened this criticism, especially by emphasizing the sinful character of all institutions and all of society. Included in this skepticism about institutions was a critique of the church. Denominations were particularly scrutinized because they contradicted the ecumenical ideal. Too often based upon race, class, or nationalism, argued H. Richard Niebuhr, denominations represented the moral failure of Christianity.[26]

Neo-orthodox leaders were frequently skeptical about the religious revival of the 1950s, and popular critiques of Protestant piety and church life rolled from the presses. In *The Surge of Piety in America* (1958), A. Roy Eckardt sarcastically commented, "It is rather hard to see how we can stand very long the terrific pace our surging piety has set for itself." Other criticisms of post-war religiosity included Will Herberg's *Protestant-Catholic-Jew* (1955), Peter Berger's *The Noise of Solemn Assemblies* (1961), Gibson Winter's *The Suburban Captivity of the Churches* (1961), and Martin Marty's *The Fire We Can Light* (1959).[27]

On the eve of the 1960s, mainstream Protestant church leaders found themselves in a puzzling situation. On the one hand, the church never seemed stronger — rising membership, healthy finances, and vigorous theological discussion in both the church and the culture. Reinhold Niebuhr, after all, had been pictured on the cover of *Time* magazine. On the other hand, the church seemed too comfortable and too secure. Its piety was sentimental; its ethics were individualistic and moralistic; and denominations, it was claimed, were preoccupied with self-preservation rather than with living out the fullness and radical character of the gospel.

Neo-orthodoxy's critique of the church and society rang true during the 1950s and still remains compelling decades later. Its strength was its capacity to define Christianity in contrast to conservative Protestant theology and American culture. Neo-orthodoxy's critical perspective, however, failed to adequately address perplexing questions raised by the pluralism and relativism of modern culture. As historian Sydney Ahlstrom declared, the neo-orthodox theologians laid "a very thin sheet of dogmatic asphalt over the problems created by modern critical thought." James Moorhead, however, adds that neo-orthodoxy's affirmation of the changing character of Christian doctrine introduced "a principle of self-criticism and volatility conducive to further change."[28]

In short, neo-orthodoxy prepared the ground for a more radical theological experimentation, as well as a more rigorous critique of denominationalism and the church as an institution. In its acute defensiveness against conservative Protestantism, however, neo-orthodoxy failed to recognize the changes on the right that made some conservatives allies, rather than opponents. Taken as a whole, the intellectual world of mainstream Protestants left them ill-prepared for the massive changes they would confront in the 1960s.[29]

Some historians and interpreters of American religion and culture see the 1960s as a watershed. Sydney Ahlstrom identified it as the era of "the radical turn in theology and ethics" and the end of "a Great Puritan Epoch" in Anglo-American culture. The decade, he wrote, "was a time . . . when the old grounds of national confidence, patriotic idealism, moral traditionalism, and even of historic Judeo-Christian theism, were awash. Presuppositions that had held firm for centuries — even millennia — were being widely questioned. . . . The nation was confronting revolutionary circumstances whose effects were . . . irreversible."[30]

The Re-forming Period since the 1960s

Ahlstrom wrote at the end of the sixties. His verdict neglects earlier changes, for the forties and fifties paved the way for patterns of massive change. But the sixties and succeeding decades have transformed American culture and religion, especially its mainstream Protestant churches. Let us look more closely at "the radical turn in theology and ethics."

Theology

Measured against the previous four centuries of Christian history, the most revolutionary shift in the 1960s was Vatican II and the resulting collapse of tensions and polemics between Roman Catholics and Protestants. Convened by Pope John XXIII from 1962 to 1965 and attended by Protestant observers, Vatican II radically and irrevocably changed the course of Western Christian history. For those born after Vatican II, it is almost impossible to understand the mistrust, prejudice, and animosity that had characterized Catholic-Protestant relations since the sixteenth century.[31]

As early as the mid-1960s, books by Catholic theologians such as Karl Rahner, Hans Küng, Gregory Baum, and Pierre Teilhard de Chardin were being widely read and discussed by Protestants. Catholic biblical scholars were welcomed in what had once been exclusively Protestant circles. Raymond Brown, a prominent New Testament scholar and Catholic priest, assumed a position at Union Theological Seminary in New York in 1970, and he was not an exception. In the thirty years since Vatican II, Catholics have assumed faculty positions in many mainstream Protestant seminaries and divinity schools. Likewise, Protestants have been appointed to Catholic seminaries and universities, such as the University of Notre Dame.[32]

Vatican II unleashed powerful forces within Catholicism which continue to reverberate into the late twentieth century. Its theological implications, however, are also profound and far-reaching for mainstream Protestants. No longer can theology be understood simply as a Protestant inquiry, or the exploration of any one particular tradition — Reformed, Lutheran, Methodist, Anglican, Anabaptist, etc. Theology since the 1960s has been an investigation of the Christian tradition understood broadly; it is ecumenical in spirit and in fact. Likewise, despite the distinctive characteristics of worship in mainstream Protestantism and Catholicism, both traditions draw heavily from one another in the preparation of worship resources and in practice. In prayer and spirituality, for example, it is as acceptable for a Protestant to read the Roman Catholic Henri Nouwen as it is for a Catholic to read the Quaker Parker Palmer. In Christian education, pastoral care, and Christian ethics, Protestants and Catholics learn freely and unapologetically from one another.

In short, Vatican II and ensuing ecumenical dialogues have changed the way Christians believe, worship, pray, and minister to one another. The unique features of Protestantism or Catholicism have gradually blurred, and in their place has emerged an ecumenical vision of the church and the Christian life.

Since the 1960s a second major development has transformed theology: the emergence of new theological voices with different theological emphases. Since the prevailing theme of these new voices is freedom, they are known as liberation theologians.

The civil rights movement compelled Americans to confront racism and segregation. African American leaders and theologians, such as Martin Luther King, Jr., James H. Cone, and J. Deotis Roberts, have raised urgent and compelling questions about the church's complicity in perpetuating the oppression of African Americans.[33]

Asian, African, and Latin American theologians have challenged the adequacy of a Christian theology based entirely on Western forms of thought. Many have argued that the Bible shows "a preferential option for the poor," and not for affluent Western Christians. The gospel is a message of liberation. It brings freedom from sin, but also from economic and political oppression, particularly the oppression generated by the West.[34]

Feminist theologians — Letty Russell, Rosemary Radford Ruether, and Elizabeth Johnson, for example — have protested that Christianity has been influenced pervasively by the values of male-dominated societies. They call for a Christianity and church that abolishes both patriarchy and hierarchy as patterns of authority, that affirms the equality of men and women within the church, and that understands the mystery of God as neither male nor female.[35]

These new theological movements, with their perceptive if sometimes strident critiques, represent the most significant questioning of the church and Christianity since the Reformation. There is great diversity among the new voices in Christian theology, and some take their arguments to more radical conclusions than others.

At stake in these debates is not only the moral integrity of the church but also the moral integrity of Christianity itself. The church must not simply be reformed, many of these theologians declare; Christian theology itself must be reconceived. To use the controversial term from a 1993 ecumenical conference on women, God and the church must be "re-imagined."

A third movement in mainstream Protestant theology — interdisciplinary methodology — has introduced even more diversity by drawing on other disciplines and experimenting with various theological methods. Theologians have borrowed from a variety of academic fields and schools of thought — sociology, phenomenology, literary criticism, psychology, process philosophy, linguistics, communication theory, and more. The results have been intriguing and sometimes exciting. But the interest in and enthusiasm for these theological experiments have been confined largely to academic circles. Because the literature is technical and specialized, this theology remains in the domain of professionals and has had little impact on the life of the church.[36]

In thirty years, theology has changed from an inquiry by white, Western, and predominantly male theologians working with Western philosophical concepts into a much broader, richer, and more complex discussion of the nature of God and the world. Its participants are now both men and women, drawn from the Christian church spanning the globe.

Ethics

Theological issues have spawned lively controversies in mainstream Protestantism since the 1960s. The most wrenching issues, however, have been posed by the rethinking of Christian ethics. There is or should be a close relationship between theology and ethics, and the "radical turn" has introduced emotional and sometimes divisive debates about ethics into mainstream Protestantism. The questions have been posed, in part, by those who seek to reformulate Christian belief, and particularly by those who recognize dramatic changes in American society and the world.

Initially, post–World War II debates involved racial justice. As the civil rights movement escalated both its tactics and its rhetoric, the largely white mainstream Protestant denominations became acutely aware of deep-seated racism in American society and in the churches. The pain was particularly intense in the South. Like the Civil War, the confrontation with racism divided families, congregations, communities, and occasionally denominations. The preaching and leadership of Martin Luther King, Jr., as well as other African American ministers, was especially powerful because its assault on racism was based on explicitly Christian and American democratic traditions. At the heart of the civil rights movement was an indictment of America as a racist nation, as well as a plea for America to embody Christian and democratic ideals by creating liberty and justice for all of its citizens.[37]

Mainstream Protestants found it difficult and painful to accept the responsibility and guilt for the racism of American society — even though they had shaped that racism to a great degree. Their leaders eventually did provide critical political leverage in passing the civil rights legislation during the 1960s. But the burden of guilt was heavy. As Presbyterian Eugene Carson Blake admitted at the March on Washington in 1963, "We come and late we come." Race was so highly charged in southern congregations that pastors or priests found that references to "brotherhood" or "justice" or "freedom" in worship were heard as codes for endorsing civil rights. Decades after the height of the civil rights movement, one white pastor in Birmingham, Alabama, declared, "It finally was a relief; it taught us how to be Christian again."[38]

At the same time that Americans were confronting the racism in their society, the idea of America's political innocence was also under attack. One of the staples of American national identity has been a belief that Americans were a chosen people, selected by God for a particular mission — the creation of liberty and justice. Americans were taught by preachers and politicians that the United States enjoyed a special relationship with God. Particularly in foreign affairs, American policies were seen to be noble and enlightened because they were based on moral principles, not on national self-interest.[39]

Neo-orthodox theologians had criticized this alliance of Christianity and nationalism during World War II. The mainstream Protestant endorsement of that war was therefore careful and measured, especially by comparison with other wars in American history. However, the Vietnam War dramatically undermined the notion of America's innocence and its moral role in world affairs. For the first time in American history, the mainstream Protestant denominations issued major indictments of the U.S. and its war policies.[40]

Mainstream Protestant churches have never been pacifist or "peace churches," rejecting war in all cases on moral grounds. After the explosion of the atomic bomb, however, and during the Vietnam War, a growing "peace lobby" in these denominations prompted a vigorous and continuing debate over the ethics of any war fought for any reason.[41]

Vietnam also sparked a sharply critical attitude toward America's economic involvement in other areas of the world, as well as criticism of the capitalist system itself. A few Social Gospel leaders had questioned the morality of business, and occasionally even capitalism itself, as early as the late nineteenth century. Deeper and more pointed criticisms emerged during the Great Depression, and by mid-century some theologians saw great promise in Marxism for Christian theology and ethics. While the critique of capitalism never fared well in many mainstream Protestant congregations, it often found a voice among theologians and denominational leaders. Those who had both experience working in the Third World and knowledge of liberation theology were especially critical of American capitalism, seeing it as a form of economic imperialism.[42]

The challenges to national identity posed by racism, war, and economics have shaken American culture — especially the mainstream Protestant churches. Even more explosive have been issues involving families, gender, and human sexuality.

Since the 1960s, divorce in America has escalated dramatically.

In 1960, there were 26 divorces for every 100 marriages; by 1990 the rate had nearly doubled to 48 divorces for every 100 marriages. This does not mean, however, that half of all marriages end in divorce; some individuals have multiple divorces. Approximately one-quarter of all marriages do end in divorce, and the rate has been stable since the late 1970s. As divorce increasingly affected families in mainstream Protestant congregations, churches gradually relaxed their disapproval of divorce while still seeking to support families and marriages. Since the 1960s, marriage and family counseling has become a growth industry among mainstream Protestant ministers.[43]

During the 1960s, the second wave of feminism emerged in America, particularly among well-educated white women. The first wave was the woman's suffrage movement of the nineteenth and early twentieth centuries. The new feminists' quest for equality in employment, their rejection of a "woman's role" at home and with children, and their search for justice for women under the law involved more than legislative and economic change. Contemporary feminists called for far-reaching changes in the relationships between men and women, and they demanded transformed structures of authority and power in both church and society.[44]

Fueling these heated issues were two epochal changes — one in science, one in law. Birth control pills appeared in the 1960s. For the first time in human history, women had the power to control their reproduction — safely and effectively. In 1973, the Supreme Court legalized abortion. In both instances, women were provided with freedom to choose not to give birth — by preventing conception, or by stopping the development of a fertilized egg. Choice, which was transforming so many areas of American society, was now available to women and families in deciding whether or not to have children and how many children to have. Like so many of the controversies since the 1960s, the abortion debate is focused on rights — the right of the mother to choose, the right of the fetus to live. But what science and the law had granted, above all, was the opportunity for sexually active women to make a choice about pregnancy.[45]

Abortion continues to be an emotional and controversial issue in American society, shaping its politics and dividing its churches.

But the use of artificial means of birth control is widely accepted by both Protestants and Catholics. By the mid-1990s, most mainstream Protestant denominations had reached the position that abortion is a tragedy, but in some cases it is an ethical way to resolve difficult and irresolvable alternatives.[46]

Sexuality itself has also been a focus of controversy. It is impossible to know the sexual behavior of earlier generations, but since the 1960s American society has become more relaxed about sexual behavior both prior to and outside of marriage. Mainstream Protestants have debated the ethics of moral standards regarding sex — particularly in light of studies revealing the high levels of sexual activity among young people. Since sexual standards and sexual behavior seem dramatically divergent, churches argue about whether Christian teaching on sexual ethics ought to change.[47]

By the 1990s, homosexuality dominated the ethical agendas of nearly all the mainstream Protestant churches. Lutherans, United Methodists, Episcopalians, and Presbyterians have been engaged in heated debates over policies that would soften or remove the church's condemnation of homosexual behavior and that would allow the ordination of homosexuals as ministers. Like all sexual behavior, homosexuality is controversial because it involves the most intimate area of human life and human identity. For Christians, it also raises questions about the authority of the Bible and the church's historic teachings.

Jann Martin, a Lutheran in Michigan, captured the anguished' moral conscience of many mainstream Protestants as she discussed her denomination's debate over homosexuality in the 1990s. She agreed that discrimination against homosexuals in housing or employment was wrong. She often participated in discussions of homosexuality in her congregation. But ordaining homosexuals or supporting same-sex unions was going too far, she maintained. "I do not agree that just because the times are changing, we should change our morals."[48]

This is the dilemma for mainstream Protestants: Do changing times assume changing morals?

Since the 1960s mainstream Protestants have grappled with the idea of their nation as racist and imperialist. They have agonized as their families divided and as sexual mores changed. They have

c

encouraged women to embrace equality and have ordained them
to positions of leadership. They have found that homosexuality
affected them — either in their own families or through someone
close to them.

They have been instructed by theologians and ethicists to "be
open," and they have heeded the call. But by the end of the
twentieth century, mainstream Protestants are asking whether there
are limits to openness, whether there are boundaries to Christian
faith and ethics — boundaries which ought to be drawn to resist
the capriciousness of unreflective or unlimited choice.

The outcome of the re-forming period in theology and ethics
is not clear. The full implications of "the radical turn" in theology
and ethics are ambiguous. Mainstream Protestant churches find
themselves as disestablished churches — one choice among many
— competing for the values of their members and the society.

What is certain is that their willingness to engage the pluralism
of Christian belief, religious diversity, and differences in values
makes them distinctive among Christian communities.[49] If mainstream Protestants are able to deal with the pluralism of their world
without eroding their Christian identity, they will help forge a vision
of Christian belief and behavior that will make a powerful and
constructive contribution to the global church in the twenty-first
century.

4. Nurturing Faith: The Ecosystems of Mainstream Protestantism

ALL religious communities try to transmit their beliefs and values from one generation to another. During the nineteenth century, mainstream Protestants launched a vast enterprise to nurture the Christian faith in their members and to communicate it to others outside their churches.

To use one helpful image, mainstream Protestants created an "ecosystem" of institutions and practices — both formal and informal — which undergirded Christian commitment and faith. The elements of nature's ecosystem — plants, animals, food, water, and air — live in a dynamic equilibrium. While constantly in flux on the surface, their interaction over time exhibits certain consistent underlying patterns that sustain the system. However, radical changes in one or more elements in the system produce severe, often unforeseen consequences throughout the rest of the system, and often precipitate crises.[1]

The nineteenth-century ecosystems of mainstream Protestantism worked according to a similar dynamic equilibrium. Created out of old and newly formed practices, these ecosystems sought first to capture American culture for Christ, and secondly to perpetuate the transmission of Christian beliefs, values, and church affiliation.

The changes in American culture and mainstream Protestantism in the twentieth century have decisively altered the parts and

59

patterns of its ecosystem. These disruptions have left these churches less able to transmit faith to their members, and have challenged them to reformulate an ecology for nurturing faith — an ecology analogous to the one used by their nineteenth-century forebears.

The history of these changes illumines vital signs in mainstream Protestantism that can be used in a new ecology. At the same time, analysis of these changes sharply focuses the barriers that any such new ecology will face.

Mainstream Protestant Ecosystems:
The Methodist Case

Each denominational family in mainstream Protestantism developed its own ecosystem for nurturing and spreading its particular understanding of the Christian faith. Consider, for example, the ideal case of young Methodists in the early 1900s.[2]

These Methodist families held family devotions at least once a week — on Sunday, if not daily. They attended Sunday school and church on Sunday morning and worshiped again on Sunday evening. They set time aside for the Wednesday evening prayer meeting. Late summer revivals — during the "lay by time" between hoeing and harvesting — were supplemented by special Easter, Christmas, and Mother's Day celebrations. "Aldersgate Sunday," the closest Sabbath to May 24, was another high point for worship in the Methodist ecosystem. The service marked the time when John Wesley felt his heart "strangely warmed," and Methodists were encouraged to participate in the same experience, and invite others to do the same.

Those raised in Methodism "joined the church" at puberty and attended the Epworth League, Intermediates, and then Seniors from the seventh to the twelfth grade. Along with members of their families, the youth read *The Christian Advocate,* a denominational journal with a large circulation.

Those who went to college often selected a Methodist college or university — such as Wesleyan in Connecticut or Ohio or Kentucky, Northwestern in Illinois, Vanderbilt in Tennessee, Syracuse in New York, the University of Southern California, or one of the other Methodist schools across the nation. There they enrolled in required religion courses, in addition to courses in the arts, humanities, and sciences. The faculty members were overwhelmingly Christian and predominantly Methodist. Many students joined the Methodist college student organization, the Wesley Foundation. Some non-Methodists became members during their college years through revivals or other evangelistic endeavors. Many students enlisted in mission or service projects sponsored by the Methodists or the YMCA or YWCA.

When they became adults, men and women joined associations set aside for them within a congregation but organized across the denomination. This was particularly true of Methodist women's groups. The Methodist Women's Foreign Mission Society and the Methodist Women's Home Mission society had circles or small group meetings, projects, and leadership development courses. Similarly, men belonged to the Methodist Brotherhood.

Congregations belonged to a circuit and gathered each season for Quarterly Conference, a time to do business but also a time for worship together. Annual Conferences gathered Methodist pastors from several districts. Pastors stood, publicly reported on their charges, and presented their apportionment of benevolent funds. Laypeople also attended this clergy-dominated event full of preaching and ecclesiastical deliberations to learn about the church and its mission around the world.

Minor differences existed between the Methodist Episcopal Church and the Methodist Episcopal Church, South. Members of the former read *The Epworth Herald,* while members of the latter read *The Epworth Era.* African American Methodists developed not only their own denominations but their own schools: Shaw University in North Carolina, Claflin College in South Carolina, and Clark College in Georgia. Through their congregations and schools, black and white Methodists forged two separate ecosystems of faith.

Other mainstream Protestant denominations played variations on this theme, adding their own distinctive emphases. These denominations also depended on one another for mutual support. A Methodist college might well include a Presbyterian and an Episcopalian on its board of trustees. It would welcome a sizeable minority of its students from other mainstream Protestant backgrounds; yet it would make few concessions to them. The college would appeal for financial support across denominational lines. A Baptist conference center would schedule Disciples of Christ meetings on a regular basis. Several congregations from different denominations would collaborate in sponsoring a school for Mexican Americans or a seminary in Puerto Rico.[3]

Despite the variations among these denominations, there were common elements in the mainstream Protestant ecosystem: family worship, Sunday schools, worship, special groups for every age, many forms of mission, church-related colleges and universities, seminaries, camps, conferences, and so on. The ecosystem provided institutions and programs for every stage of life, binding individuals to the denomination. Binding people even more closely to the church were the ties of family and kinship. Each element reinforced congregational life and denominational loyalty. The ecology shaped the way people thought, prayed, and behaved. A closer examination of these elements demonstrates both the dynamism and the waning of the Protestant ecosystem in the twentieth century as well as the challenge of strengthening its vitality in a changing culture.

Family Devotions, the Sunday School, and the Sabbath

At the turn of the century, mainstream Protestant leaders talked about three institutions indispensable for Christian nurture: family devotions, the Sunday school, and the Christian Sabbath.

The most important institution was the practice of family devotions — the nurturing of Christian faith within families. Prior to the arrival of the Sunday school, the family was the primary means of transmitting faith from one generation to the next. Even in the late nineteenth century, members of the household gathered for Bible reading, prayer, and singing hymns. Christian doctrine or church matters were openly discussed around the dinner table. Parents blessed food before it was eaten; the day ended with bedtime prayers. In denominations that used catechisms, parents frequently guided children in memorizing the answers to the questions of faith.[4]

How many actually practiced such family piety? It is impossible to know, but there is enough evidence to suggest that it was widespread — as an ideal and in reality. Most denominations had mechanisms for reinforcing the practice of family devotions. Presbyterians included a separate section on family worship in their "Directory for Worship" and used a "Family Altar Pledge"; families who signed the pledge card promised that they would read the Bible and pray daily during the year.[5]

The link between the home and Christianity in the Protestant ecology of faith was crucial. Historian Colleen McDannell asserts that family worship "was a teaching ritual. Although praise, thanksgiving, and petitioning were important in family worship, prayer took a backseat to instruction from the Bible, especially in the evangelical churches. . . . Reading from the Bible constantly reminded the family of the religious goals which they pursued. Daily reference to that instruction, whether through scriptural readings or the telling of biblical tales, was essential to Protestant domestic worship."[6]

The second indispensable institution of Christian nurture was what mainstream Protestants termed "the Christian Sabbath." Pastors and other leaders enjoined their parishioners to remember the commandment in Exodus 20:8-11 ("Remember the Sabbath, and keep it holy . . ."). They linked the Sabbath to the culmination of the creation story in Genesis 2:2-3, where God rested on the seventh day and hallowed it. They were reminded, however, that Jesus had resisted the legalism of Sabbath observance, healing on that day and allowing the hungry disciples to eat. Protestants supported similar "deeds of necessity and mercy" in their own day. They read and believed the Acts of the Apostles, where the early church gathered on the first day of the week, Sunday, as the "Lord's Day," and they expected everyone to assume the same interpretation of Scripture.[7]

Mainstream Protestant churches collaborated in communities across the nation to pass and enforce laws that kept people from working on Sunday. They conceded that cows needed milking — but factories did not have to operate. Doctors could deliver babies — but mail did not have to be delivered. Connecticut, a bastion of Protestant strength at the turn of the century, passed a model law for Sabbath observance and printed it on blue paper. When the law was copied elsewhere, the "blue laws" received their name.[8]

The Protestant Sabbath was too often defined in negative terms: "Thou shalt not. . . ." It was a time of not reading the secular newspapers, not engaging in commerce, not taking excursions, sometimes not even cooking. In positive terms, however, the Protestant Sabbath was a time of preparing for worship, worshiping, visiting the sick, and reading Christian literature. It was a time for rest and reflection. It was a time for God, families, and friends.

The Sabbath was a means of providing rhythm to life. It signified in concrete terms that one's lifestyle was informed by one's commitment to God.

The Protestant Sabbath was an attempt to order life by creating sacred time — an impulse common to all religions. Its power is evident in eighteenth- and nineteenth-century American culture. In the early settlement of Kentucky, for example, one Jane Stevenson remembered that her wagon train stopped on Saturday early enough to cook everything necessary for the Sabbath. It remained in place through Sunday, despite the threat of Indian attack and the settlers' desire to stake their claims as quickly as possible in the Bluegrass. Presbyterian Albert Barnes, a minister in Philadelphia, believed so strongly in Sabbath observance that he would start a new congregation in Philadelphia whenever his congregation expanded so much that its members could not walk to worship on Sunday. For Barnes, Sabbath observance meant people should not use transportation on the Lord's Day.[9]

Obviously, not everyone shared this Protestant enthusiasm for the Sabbath. Roman Catholics rejected the idea of stripping the day of human pleasures. Their "Continental Sabbath" allowed for family gatherings and play, including the consumption of alcohol. Jewish leaders, augmented by Seventh Day Baptists and Adventists, objected that Saturday, rather than Sunday, should be the legally recognized day of worship and praise. When these cases entered the courts, mainstream Protestant leaders based their appeal for Sunday as the Sabbath on the ground of America as "a Christian nation."

Yet these efforts failed, partly because even rank-and-file Protestants themselves were losing enthusiasm for a day whose requirements they increasingly viewed as restrictive, negative, and legalistic. As strict Sabbath observance began to disappear in the 1920s and 1930s, most mainstream Protestants welcomed its demise and considered the overthrow of "blue laws" as a sign of reform.[10]

The third important institution of Christian nurture was the Sunday school. At the turn of the twentieth century, the Sunday school was in its heyday, still guided by lay Christians who led the singing, gathered the children in assemblies, divided them into carefully graded classes frequently segregated by gender, and taught the faith using Bible stories and their own experience. They sought to reach the children of the poor and the unchurched, and provided instruction for the children of the congregation. The primary purpose of the nineteenth-century Sunday school was evangelism; Christian nurture of the faithful complemented this emphasis. The Sunday school also included classes for men and women, taught by respected leaders and usually focusing on mission, drawing moral examples from the Bible.[11]

Sunday school teachers and superintendents gathered for training, both locally and nationally. International gatherings were frequently led by businessmen and respected public figures. Children from racial-ethnic minority groups were targeted in programs sponsored by churches and chapels on Sunday afternoons. Classes were held sometimes in the churches and sometimes in the early settlement houses. Camps and conferences strengthened the work of the Sunday school with focused, often intense, meetings which called people to conversion and to mission.[12]

The Sunday school had obvious weaknesses. The Bible studies could become lessons in simple moralisms; the theology of the teachers might be shallow and unsophisticated; the quality of teaching varied widely. Covert and open conflict between ministers and lay leaders marked the development of the Sunday school. In the early twentieth century, various denominational departments and boards of Christian education spent energy trying to regularize the raucous Sunday schools. They standardized curriculum materials and developed standards for more effective teaching. In the process they also weakened what may have been the primary benefit of the early Sunday school — namely, teachers sharing their personal faith with students.[13]

Worship and Hymnody

On Sundays, congregations offered their members the "eleven o'clock" service, or some variation of that sacred time, each with its own distinctive denominational emphases. Episcopalians and Lutherans worshiped within well-developed liturgical structures, inherited from their European ancestors, and they employed music in singing the liturgy. Among the other mainstream Protestant churches, the service was liturgically spare during the late nineteenth and early twentieth centuries, but it had its own structure and order. At the heart of Sunday worship was the reading of Scripture and the sermon, a pastoral prayer, and hymns. Among the Disciples of Christ, worship included a weekly celebration of the Lord's Supper; among Methodists, communion was received at the rail, but less frequently. Among Presbyterians and Congregationalists, a public prayer of confession was often followed by an assurance of pardon.[14]

For most mainstream Protestants, the sermon was the high point of Sunday worship. But for some, like the Episcopalians, the sermon and the Lord's Supper together formed the culmination of worship. During the late nineteenth and early twentieth centuries, preaching was extraordinarily popular, and preachers enjoyed significant influence and prestige. The best-known preachers were often referred to as "the princes of the pulpit"; they "filled" pulpits. Publishers provided a steady stream of collected sermons for the public.[15]

Most mainstream Protestant sermons had a classic evangelical format: exposition of a text and an appeal to commit one's life to Jesus Christ. Increasingly, however, preachers developed sermons around a particular theme, rather than expositing a text. During the early twentieth century, Congregationalist minister and Social Gospel leader Washington Gladden developed a preaching strategy for nurturing his congregation and expanding their social awareness. On Sunday mornings, his sermons were characteristically evangelical in nature. On Sunday evenings, he preached on social problems, new literary movements, or contemporary thinkers.[16]

Sunday worship was supplemented by other occasions of regular worship — Sunday evenings and/or Wednesday evenings, special services or revivals once or twice a year, and worship during

Sunday school assemblies or "Rally Days." Frequently led by lay people, these services were informal and even exuberant in denominations not known for such extroverted worship. Indeed, in many cases the alternative worship services satisfied a need for a more emotional and personal approach to faith, in contrast to the intellectual and aesthetic approach normally present in Sunday worship.

The varieties of evangelicalism were reflected in congregations' hymnbooks. Sunday morning services used a more formal and traditional hymnbook; Sunday evening and informal services used another hymnbook which included more gospel songs.[17]

In the early twentieth century, mainstream Protestants sang a wide variety of hymns. Episcopalians and Lutherans used their own distinctive tradition of hymnody, which partially overlapped into other mainstream Protestant denominations. Methodists included hymns from their Anglican heritage, but their hymnals were laden with hymns by Charles Wesley and other representatives of the "singing Methodists" — Ira Sankey, Fanny Crosby, W. P. Bliss, and other Wesleyans. In other mainstream Protestant churches, the hymnody drew on both high and low church traditions, but the hymns of eighteenth- and nineteenth-century evangelicalism predominated.[18]

By the turn of the twentieth century, two subtle but significant changes in hymns were evident. First, the emphasis upon human sin declined in favor of God's benevolent love for humanity. For example, a popular children's hymnbook published by Presbyterians in 1852 included this characteristic Calvinist statement of human depravity:

> I know that I was born in sin,
> I feel much evil work within,
> Sins that offend my Maker's eyes,
> Dwell in my heart and often rise.[19]

By 1900, Presbyterian and other mainstream Protestants were more apt to sing another hymn, which proclaimed:

> What a Friend we have in Jesus, all our sins and griefs to bear!
> What a privilege to carry everything to God in prayer.

O what peace we often forfeit, O what needless pain we bear,
All because we do not carry everything to God in prayer.[20]

A worship of God who loves rather than judges would become increasingly evident in Protestant piety during the twentieth century.[21]

A second theme of triumph appeared in the mission hymns of the late nineteenth and early twentieth century. These hymns captured mainstream Protestants' confidence in the progressive triumph of both Christian missions and Western civilization:

Light of the world, we hail Thee, flushing the eastern skies,
Never shall darkness veil Thee again from human eyes;
Too long, alas, withholden, now spread from shore to shore;
Thy light, so glad and golden, shall set on earth no more.

Light of the world, illumine this darkened earth of Thine,
Till everything that's human be filled with what's divine;
Till every tongue and nation, from sin's dominion free,
Rise in the new creation which springs from love and Thee.[22]

Education and Social Service

The mainstream Protestant ecosystems thrived on a vast educational network constructed during the nineteenth century. Its most visible component was the church-related college. Prior to the Civil War, Presbyterians and Congregationalists led in establishing institutions of higher education. Eventually, however, the Methodists founded more colleges and universities than any other denomination. At the turn of the century, nearly half of the undergraduates were enrolled in church-related colleges, most of which were formally affiliated with mainstream Protestant denominations.[23]

In the early 1900s, mainstream Protestants also developed a new venture in higher education — campus ministry. Campus pastors or priests were placed not only in church-related colleges but also on the campuses of public universities. Presbyterians led the way; between 1905 and 1909 they established their presence at universities in Kansas, Illinois, Wisconsin, Colorado, Arkansas, and

Nebraska. Other denominations followed suit. They sponsored ministries for their own students and any others who wished to join.[24]

Church-related colleges and campus ministries helped sustain denominational loyalty and provided a feeder system for the church's lay and ministerial leadership. Although there are few studies to confirm this, it is likely that until World War II the vast majority of mainstream Protestant ministers graduated from church-related colleges. These institutions also provided a significant form of evangelism for mainstream Protestants, drawing students into the orbit of a particular denomination during the formative college years.[25]

Denominational seminaries were another critical aspect of mainstream Protestantism's ecosystem. Some denominations were slower than others in requiring a seminary degree for ordination, but it gradually became the norm in the twentieth century. Although Union Seminary in New York and the divinity schools at Yale, Harvard, and Chicago educated many mainstream Protestant ministers during the first half of the twentieth century, the vast majority of mainstream Protestant ministers were educated in their own denomination's seminaries.[26]

Although higher education was essential to the mainstream Protestant ecosystem, the most powerful educational institutions were the public schools, or "common schools" as they were called in the nineteenth century. Nearly every mainstream Protestant denomination experimented with church-sponsored primary and secondary schools. Only the Lutherans and Episcopalians, however, created a system of day schools that continues into the late twentieth century. Mainstream Protestants effectively seized control of America's public education during the nineteenth century. Indeed, this is one of the best indications that they were, in effect, "established" churches.[27]

Mainstream Protestantism's domination of public education extended well into the twentieth century. In 1920, a United Lutheran Church editor praised a Bible study curriculum for the Atchison, Kansas, public schools. He declared that the Bible should be studied by all children because "its truths are objective, as are the truths of history and science, and it asks no favors from the teacher." It was assumed, he added, that the teacher would be "a proper person, that is, a Christian." A Disciples of Christ editor in 1921 maintained that "our Public School needs the influence of, and the spiritual uplift of Christianity minus any touch of sectarianism." There were limits, however; no "popery" would be tolerated.[28]

Public school administrators listened to these appeals and implemented them. One Indiana county consistently offered Bible courses in all of its ten high schools throughout the 1920s. In 1944 more than twenty thousand students were enrolled in Bible courses in approximately one hundred North Carolina towns. At the same time, the public schools of Kalamazoo, Michigan, provided daily Bible reading, plus daily devotions, religious drama, and Bible memory exercises.[29]

McGuffey's Readers, compiled by the Presbyterian William H. McGuffey, were especially influential in inculcating a Protestant moral tone to public education. An estimated 80 percent of all public school children used these books from 1837 to the early twentieth century. From these readers they received lessons on the value of work, honesty, loyalty, Sabbath observance, and the dangers of alcohol.[30]

Roman Catholic and Jewish people responded to the Protestant hold on public education by founding their own educational systems — elementary and secondary schools, colleges, and seminaries. Schools for racial-ethnic minorities, some of which were public and others founded by churches, also provided a steady dose of Protestant piety.[31] Racial-ethnic minority leaders of mainstream Protestant denominations frequently came from these church-based schools — which provided a close-knit connection within minority communities. "We learned to look out for one another," said one Presbyterian denominational executive.

As the Protestant faith ecosystem took form during the nineteenth century, faith and education reinforced one another. Mainstream Protestants operated with a firm assumption: the life of the mind and the life of the spirit were one.

The Protestant ecosystem also included a network of social service institutions and organizations designed to address a wide range of social needs and problems. These included hospitals, orphanages, homes for the elderly, rescue missions, and other institutions. Mainstream Protestants were especially active in promoting the work of the YMCA and YWCA during the first half of the twentieth century when the "Y" movement had an explicitly Protestant and evangelistic orientation.[32] All of these activities grew out of the mainstream Protestant conviction that faith should produce acts of charity and love which contribute to righteousness in society.

As was the case in education, Roman Catholic and Jewish people established a comparable system of charities and social service institutions. Similarly, African American Christians created their own service organizations to deal with segregation in rural and urban communities. Unlike their mainstream Protestant counterparts, however, these institutions did not shed their religious affiliation and identity in the twentieth century.[33]

Beginning with the New Deal during the 1930s, American society developed a welfare state in which government, rather than the private sector, became the dominant source of social services in every community. But prior to the 1930s, social services were provided largely by churches and synagogues. Consequently, social service institutions were products of Jewish, Roman Catholic, and various Protestant communities. For the racial-ethnic minority communities, their own institutions symbolized both racial segregation and the energy and self-reliance of the minority communities. When the government expanded its role, and the walls between religious groups and minority groups began to crumble, the mission of religiously motivated social service agencies changed — and so did the religious ecosystems that supported them.

The Waning of the Protestant Ecosystems

By the late twentieth century, the Protestant ecosystem of faith had been disrupted and weakened in virtually every area of its life. The changes were particularly devastating for the "established" churches — the mainstream Protestant denominations. The waning of the Protestant ecosystems did not occur overnight or at a steady rate. Some parts of the ecology were threatened early in the twentieth century; other parts came under attack much later.

The many elements of the ecosystem were altered not only because of profound transformations in American society, but also because the churches intentionally changed the ecosystem itself. The shifts were advocated as reforms by well-intentioned and idealistic people who did not fully appreciate the importance of the ecosystem, and who believed the church had grown beyond some of its earlier practices. In some cases, they were right; but, as we shall see, these changes had unintended consequences.

Consider, for example, the three core institutions — family worship, the Sunday school, and the Christian Sabbath. The fate of family worship is perhaps the most important shift in the Protestant ecosystem of faith during this century. The family had remained the primary context for Christian nurture throughout the nineteenth century. In the early twentieth century, however, mainstream Protestant churches increasingly stressed the role of *both* families and the Sunday school for communicating the Christian faith from generation to generation. By the mid-twentieth century, parents increasingly delegated the responsibility of nurturing faith to the Sunday school alone, and gave it one or two hours a week in which to accomplish this essential task.[34]

We do not know when families began to neglect religious practices such as family devotions. What is clear is that many mainstream Protestant families no longer discuss or practice religion within the family setting. Family devotions, family religious practices, and even family conversation have become the exception, rather than the norm. For example, one recent study of mainstream Protestant adolescents revealed that 64 percent never or rarely participated in family devotions. A majority of these teens never or rarely talked with their fathers about religion and God; approximately one-third experienced the same lack with their mothers.[35]

Why has the role of the family in nurturing faith declined in mainstream Protestantism? Part of the answer unquestionably lies in the changing character of the American family itself — more mobility, more divorce, more parental employment, more pressures, fewer children, and less time together.

This transformation of American families has been paralleled by changes in American values, especially attitudes and policies toward children. As Marian Wright Edelman, the founder and president of the Children's Defense Fund, has written: "What are the true values of a wealthy, democratic nation that lets infants and toddlers be the poorest group of citizens? . . . How does one reconcile rampant national child neglect and preventable suffering with the biblical warning that from those to whom much is given, much is expected?"[36]

But the decline of the religious role of the family in mainstream Protestant churches is ultimately due to subtle but significant changes in church members themselves. The parents of the baby boomers were often seeking freedom from a spirituality in their past which they saw as moralistic and coercive. They refused to impose religious disciplines upon their children, forgetting that the forms of such piety could be changed while maintaining the disciplines of the Christian life.

Mainstream Protestant churches encouraged this rejection of a Christianity understood as moral guidelines and pietistic practice. In doing so, they silently ignored families as a means of Christian nurture and accepted the increased responsibility for nurturing children's Christianity through the Sunday school.

As mainstream Protestant denominational leaders confronted the 1960s, they responded by calling for a significant shift in priorities. Benton Johnson describes this shift as a move from "the old agenda" of concern for family and personal morals to "the new agenda" focusing on corporate and systemic evils in society.[37] Concern for families never disappeared completely from mainstream Protestantism, especially within its congregations. But since the 1960s, denominations have neglected families and family life as priorities. The shift occurred just as families themselves entered a period of unprecedented change and as parents were delegating the Christian formation of their children to Sunday schools and congregations.[38]

For nearly all mainstream denominations, the Sunday school became the church school, led by professionals rather than laypeople. The emergence of Directors of Christian Education allowed pastors or priests to withdraw from the province of the Sunday school. Beginning in the 1930s, the mainstream Protestant denominations became acutely aware of insights from psychology and other social sciences and the significance of historical criticism of

the Bible. Neo-orthodox theology raised new questions and accented different themes in the Christian faith. After World War II,
mainstream Protestant churches responded to the changing environment affecting the Sunday school. From their presses flowed
books and Christian education curriculum material, sophisticated
in both theology and educational theory.[39]

These curriculum materials of mainstream Protestantism are
fascinating yet understudied. In examining the twentieth-century
Presbyterian material, Craig Dykstra and Bradley Wigger found a
shift from the student to the teacher and from message to method.
Deliberations on the delivery of education triumphed over the
content of what should be or could be learned. Dykstra and Wigger
concluded that the Presbyterian Christian education material
"gradually replaced books, tracts, and stories as the Sunday School's
basic literature." "Indeed," they wrote, "it can be argued that over
time it also replaced the Bible. Thus the enormous variety of
literature and styles that had been in the hands of teachers and
students was reduced significantly, and the control of the literature
was held more tightly by the denomination." The goal of Christian
instruction also gradually shifted from encouraging a commitment
to the Christian faith to acquiring knowledge of the content of
faith.[40]

Congregations and their Sunday school teachers eventually
rebelled. While no denomination ever achieved universal support
for its Christian education curricula, approval was sufficiently
strong and broad-based to make Sunday school curricula the "cash
cow" of mainstream Protestant publishing houses during the
1950s and early 1960s. Since the mid-1960s, however, mainstream
Protestant congregations have exercised more freedom of choice,
selecting materials from their own denomination, from other
churches (including Roman Catholicism), and from independent
publishers.[41]

The rebellion against denominationally controlled curricula
was probably due to the resistance of lay teachers. Ironically, the
"better" the curriculum became, the more difficult it was to teach.
What had been a closed market within each denomination became
an open and hotly competitive environment. The diverse and eclec-
tic character of Christian education materials is one reason why

congregations find it increasingly difficult to communicate a consistent view of the Christian faith, as well as the characteristic features of a denomination.

If the challenges to the Sunday school were significant, the threat to Sunday itself was even greater. The notion of Sabbath observance, culturally accepted and legally established in the early twentieth century, has almost vanished from American society. Its only genuine remnant is the absence of mail delivery on Sundays. A newspaper in a midwestern town long noted for the persistence of Sabbath observance noted the change with a front-page article in 1994, headlined: "Day of rest faces test." The article recounted the experience of a man who moved to the town five years earlier. He explained to his neighbors that his job involved working six days a week and asked if they would mind if he cut his lawn on Sunday. Their response: "As long as you don't mow it at midnight."[42]

Sabbath observance, at least as most Protestants of the nineteenth century defined it, declined for many reasons — the rise of the American "weekend" as a time of recreation and excursion, the expansion of business to seven days a week, two spouses working outside the home, and the competing claims of Judaism and various Christian churches which did not celebrate the Sabbath on Sunday. But the most powerful reason for decline was that Protestants, especially mainstream Protestants, stopped believing in the sanctity of the Sabbath.

Benton Johnson has pored through Presbyterian proclamations about the Sabbath from the early twentieth century. He notes that the proclamations became shorter and shorter, and finally stopped entirely in the 1930s. Like other mainstream Protestants, Presbyterians "dropped the subject" of the Sabbath. Its restrictions outweighed its benefits.[43]

The powerful civil buttress to the Protestant ecosystems — public education — also weakened in influence during the twentieth century. For nearly 150 years, mainstream Protestants had relied upon the public schools to be nurseries of Protestant piety. The famous school prayer case of *Engel v. Vitale* in 1962 symbolically marked the end of Christian domination of public schools. Since then, the Supreme Court has been especially careful to maintain "a wall of separation" between religion and publicly financed education, thereby shattering the synthesis of Protestantism and public education in American culture.[44]

The network of Protestant higher education was similarly transformed by design, necessity, and accident. During the late nineteenth century, leaders of American colleges and universities adopted the ideal of the university as the standard for higher education. This included an emphasis upon reason as the source for truth, and science as the method for obtaining knowledge. Within church-related colleges and universities, reformers urged that higher education resist the influence of the churches, and increase the academic freedom of inquiry which was unfettered by religious values or truth claims. By the mid-twentieth century, this reform movement had largely succeeded in reducing and restricting church influence in church-related higher education.[45]

Accelerating the process was the educational institutions' need for increased financial support and additional students. Foundations, such as the Carnegie Foundation, took a dim view of colleges where church influence was high. Institutions responded by reducing denominational power over board and faculty appointments, curriculum, and student life. Denominations could not keep pace with the escalating costs of maintaining and increasing the academic quality of their colleges and universities. After World War II, mainstream Protestant parents, even those who were graduates of denominational schools, encouraged their children to attend a school of their own choice, rather than the institutions of their church.[46]

What truly ended Protestant domination of higher education in the twentieth century was the explosion of public higher education after World War II. This expansion was fueled by the federal support of GIs seeking higher education, as well as a nationwide competition with the Soviet Union sparked by the Sputnik space probe in 1957. Federal and state governments vastly expanded their role in higher education. Colleges and universities became a growth industry in the American economy. In 1950, 2.6 million Americans attended institutions of higher education; in 1960 the number increased to 3.6 million; by 1970 it had exploded to 8.6 million. By 1965, two-thirds of all college students were enrolled in public, rather than private, institutions. Only one-sixth attended church colleges, and most of these were enrolled in Roman Catholic institutions.[47]

As mainstream Protestantism lost both institutional and educational influence, campus ministries also changed. Beginning in the 1950s, mainstream denominations increasingly adopted an ecumenical strategy on college campuses. This strategy was rooted in a theological commitment to present a unified Christian witness on the campuses, in a desire to reduce costs, and in the need to increase efficiency. During the 1960s, mainstream Protestant campus ministers encouraged student activism; the issues of race and war dominated their ministries on and off campus. The ecumenical strategy backfired, however, because churches had difficulty identifying with non-denominational ministries; social activism further alienated congregational support. By the 1980s, mainstream Protestant campus ministry was in disarray. For example, in 1950, the Presbyterians sponsored more than 500 campus ministries; by 1989 the number had fallen to 253. One Presbyterian leader concluded, "Campus ministry, as we have known it for forty years, and its ecumenical version over the last twenty, is over and done with."[48]

Perhaps most disturbing, some research suggests that higher education itself may be a negative factor in religious affiliation. Mainstream Protestants who go to college and graduate school are less likely to attend church or remain church members after their education; a similar pattern may exist among evangelical Protestants.[49] However, other research suggests that higher education may not be very important in predicting church attendance or affiliation.[50] Nevertheless, the fact remains that colleges and universities are secular environments, largely apathetic and occasionally hostile to the church as an institution, and indifferent to religious beliefs and values. American higher education, in which mainstream Protestants have played a significant role, has now turned against the church.[51]

Protestant social service agencies have lost their religious identity in a manner comparable to the educational institutions. The YMCA and YWCA no longer have an explicit Christian or religious purpose. Protestant hospitals have merged with one another and with secular hospitals; their mission continues to be the care and healing of sick people, but the religious basis and motivation for that mission have disappeared. The pattern is the same in homes for children, retirement homes, and other institutions of the social service network. These institutions, once forming an important part of Protestant ecosystems, have also lost their religious identity.

More troubling than the lost religious affiliation in these institutions is the lost visibility of mainstream Protestants' individual witness through serving in these institutions. Mainstream Protestants continue to embody their commitment to serve God through serving the needs of society. Most organizations where such service now occurs, however, no longer allow one to declare the religious motivations behind such work. The witness of contemporary mainstream Protestants in these institutions can be compared to the cheshire cat of Alice's wonderland: although the smile of service remains, the body of Christ behind the service has disappeared.

The Emerging Protestant Ecosystems

This survey of the waning of Protestant ecosystems may be depressing, but it is only one part of the picture. Clearly the past cannot be recreated, and parts of the Protestant ecosystems have deservedly disappeared. It is still too early to see any definitive characteristics of an emerging ecology comparable to the old Protestant ecosystems, and it is unlikely that anything so comprehensive should be or could be created. But there are vital signs: congregations and denominations are adapting to the changing cultural and religious environments of American culture.

The small group movement is clearly one element in the emerging Protestant ecosystem. According to Robert Wuthnow, the small group movement "is effecting a quiet revolution in American society." The numbers involved are staggering. Forty percent of Americans belong to a small group. These include 800,000 Sunday school classes (18–22 million people), 900,000 Bible-study groups (15–20 million people), 500,000 self-help groups (8–10 million people), 250,000 political/current events groups (5–10 million people), and 250,000 sports/hobby event groups (5–10 million people).[52]

Churches often host such groups — Alcoholics Anonymous, Al-Anon, Co-dependents Anonymous, Overeaters Anonymous, Parents Without Partners, Debtors Anonymous, Compassionate Friends, etc. The small group movement cuts across religious lines.

Mainstream Protestants, evangelicals and charismatics, Roman Catholics, Jews, and even people who hold no membership in any church or synagogue are involved. Churches obviously encourage small groups for Bible study and prayer. But another vast network of small groups is organized outside and alongside the church — neighborhood Bible study groups, prayer groups in large corporations, and women's groups formed by friendship and common contacts.[53]

The small group movement is diverse, with several important elements. Its leaders are invariably laypeople, rather than religious professionals. The desire to join a small group, especially a religious one, arises out of a quest for nurture and support and what Wuthnow calls "the deep yearning for the sacred that characterizes much of the American public."[54] Amidst the fragmentation of American culture, small groups are places where people "belong." Small groups create community. They make relatively few demands; therefore, people can choose freely both to join and to leave. Those who participate in small groups emphasize the beneficial effects on their lives — nearly always described in therapeutic terms. As one participant declared simply, "I come away stronger."[55]

Small groups obviously flourish in a society in which people exercise individual choices and seek therapy and cures for the afflictions of modern life. Wuthnow acknowledges that the movement breeds a simplistic and practical spirituality and a preoccupation with oneself and one's associates. Small group leaders are frequently obsessed with expansion — growth in numbers. But Wuthnow also suggests that small groups can have beneficial effects on religious institutions and American society by offering new avenues for exploring the nature of God and the pilgrimage of faith. Small groups, he argues, can move beyond themselves to a concern about society, and can explore the mystery of God who is larger than simply personal experience.[56]

Another element in the new Protestant ecosystem is service projects or service organizations. Like small groups, these develop both inside and alongside churches. They may be localized — a senior high youth group's trip to an inner city to paint homes, for example. But larger networks of social service have also appeared — Habitat for Humanity, Bread for the World, CROP Walks, or the Heifer Project. Nearly all appeal to the idealism and sense of adventure in young people, and they all include close relationships between youth and adults.

In a church in a county seat in Kentucky, we saw how the dynamics of social service bring new life to a congregation. Farmers comprised a sizeable percentage of this church. One Sunday in August, a senior high school girl asked during the service if she could make an announcement. The pastor consented, and she arose to say that the youth group had learned about the Heifer Project, based in Arkansas. The youth group wanted to raise $600 to buy a heifer and take it to a poor family in an Appalachian mountain community. She said there would be a car wash on Tuesday, and members of the youth group would do chores for church families to raise additional money. By September, they hoped to meet their goal.

The next Sunday, the young woman stood again and asked to make another announcement. Her request was honored. "Well," she said, "I don't know what to say. You have all pitched in, and we have almost $900 now. If a heifer costs $600, is there anybody here who will sell us two heifers for that? And by the way does anybody have a truck we could use to get them there?"

That congregation loved this experience, and it has been duplicated in countless congregations in many denominations. Youth and adults, again and again, have found common purpose and meaning by fulfilling the Christian charge to minister to the least of God's children.

The emerging Protestant ecosystems are also characterized by powerful "special purpose organizations" or "single issue groups." As the terminology implies, these are associations of people focusing on a particular cause. Every mainstream denomination has a panoply of these groups, and the causes cover the theological and political spectrum: homosexuality, abortion, peace, feminism (in all of its varieties), racial-ethnic concerns, personal and church renewal, prayer, missions, medical services at home and abroad, and more. For example, the United Church of Christ recognizes twenty-two such groups, including the Biblical Witness Fellowship, Coalition for Lesbian-Gay Concerns, Committee on Persons with Disabilities, Network for Environmental and Economic Responsibility, Christian/Jewish Dialogue Project, Marriage Encounter/UCC Expression, and United Black Christians, among others.[57]

Single-issue groups are often viewed as the cause of strife and contention in mainstream Protestant denominations. Indeed, their devotion to a particular cause and their political savvy frequently do create problems for denominations trying to maintain unity amidst considerable diversity.

At the same time, when denominations' power to retain loyalty and to impart identity has diminished, these single-issue groups give their members reasons for remaining within denominations. Their zeal and commitment also bring a vital, if fragmented, sense of mission to the churches they seek to influence and change.[58]

The small group movement, service projects, and special interest groups are not the only vital signs in the emerging ecosystems of American mainstream Protestantism. Even some of the older elements of the ecology retain a great deal of power in forming people's faith and witness. These include women's groups, men's groups, the Sunday school itself, theological seminaries, church camps, youth organizations within denominations and in parachurch groups, and more. Still other elements of the older ecology like family worship must be revived because of their role in Christian history in generating and sustaining belief in God and commitment to the church.

In whatever way future mainstream Protestant ecosystems are constructed, three insights should guide their building. First, any re-formed ecosystem should be instructed by the functions rather than the forms of the pieces that composed the nineteenth-century Protestant ecosystem. Resurrecting nineteenth-century forms of piety will not ensure the vitality of future ecosystems. But future vitality does depend on our learning about the enduring spiritual needs those earlier ecosystems addressed with some success. Those same needs must then be addressed by practices appropriate for our time.

Second, mainstream Protestant ecosystems have been weakened in their power to nurture the Christian faith because of both changes in the culture and transformations within the churches.

Third, religious vitality exists primarily in local congregations.

Any rebuilding of ecosystems of nurture must therefore begin with a focus on congregations.

Confronting these realities has been and will be difficult for mainstream Protestants. The waning of the ecosystems has occurred fairly rapidly, and as they declined, significant power shifted from denominational organizations to congregations. By the 1990s, many began to wonder what the future held for these denominational structures — the same structures that helped to create but also depended upon the ecosystems of mainstream Protestantism.

5. *The Organizational Revolution: Mainstream Protestant Denominations and Mission*

IN ONE congregation, a member of the governing board listened impatiently to a discussion about the results of studies on mainstream Protestantism. "I know what's wrong," he blurted out. "It's our denominational bureaucracy. We send our money to headquarters, and all it does is employ people. Mission never gets done. And when they do something, it isn't what we want. All they do is pass regulations on what we should do. We ought to keep that money here and hire another minister to specialize in evangelism."

Another chimed in: "The problem is we've got two different agendas in our denomination," she said. "There's one agenda for our national offices, and another for us in congregations. We're too concerned about ourselves. We ought to be supporting our mission work in the inner cities, among Native Americans, and especially in Africa, where the needs are so great."

That exchange reflects the fractured spirit of mainstream Protestant denominations. Sharp debates within denominations are a staple of their history, but by the late twentieth century, it was clear: mainstream Protestant denominations were in the throes of an organizational revolution. The locus of power — both spiritual and financial — had shifted away from national denominational organizations to congregations.

This dramatic transformation had parallels in other denominations and in other organizations, both profit and non-profit. Peter

Drucker, the influential analyst of the American economy and its institutions, describes the organizational revolution as one of the "new realities" of American culture.[1] The alteration of denominations has redefined them as organizations and reshaped how they accomplish their mission.

Like the restructuring of American corporations such as General Motors or IBM, denominations are struggling with structures, programs, and policies developed earlier in the twentieth century. Amidst intense disagreement about denominational mission, mainstream Protestants are baffled by the organizational malaise within their own churches. "The structure doesn't seem to work any more," sighed one retired pastor. "Back in the fifties, this denomination could really accomplish things. But today. . . ." His voice trailed off.

Denominations: The Past as Prologue

When Europeans settled in North America, they brought their churches with them. Nearly every group tried to recreate European patterns of church life. With the exception of the Anabaptists (the radical reformers of the sixteenth century who opposed any link between church and state) and Quakers, they assumed it was possible and desirable to reproduce the European pattern of establishment — a union of church and state. That union had been the dominant way of relating Christianity and political power in the Western world since Constantine recognized Christianity in the third century. Each kingdom had a church, and each church recognized a particular state or ruler. The model became known as "Christendom" or "Constantinian Christianity." In these cultures, there was one church. Groups that dissented were sects or heretics.

The American colonial experience broke from the Christendom model. Even though there were legally established churches in some colonies, the diversity of churches represented in the population made it impossible to talk of "the church" and then to describe everyone else as "sects." Enter the denomination — a halfway house between church and sect, and the most significant change in the understanding of the church since Constantine. The idea of denominations was based on the recognition that there is a core of essential beliefs common to all Christians and that conscientious Christians could agree to disagree about other issues, such as how worship should be structured or how a church should be governed.[2]

Enter as well the separation of church and state, codified as the First Amendment to the Constitution in 1791. The United States thus became the first nation to break with the tradition of Christendom. America became a denominational society with a secular state. Religious and political leaders grudgingly accepted religious diversity as an asset, rather than an aberration. They increasingly viewed toleration as not only a necessity but also a Christian and civic virtue.[3]

Even though the idea of denominations developed during the colonial period, denominations *as organizations* scarcely existed. For example, Congregationalists and Baptists who believed in congregational polity spent little time organizing anything other than new congregations. Presbyterians began their migration to the colonies in the seventeenth century. They never bothered to create a presbytery until 1706; the first synod was formed in 1716; and the first meeting of their General Assembly was delayed until 1787. Even Anglicans (or Episcopalians as they are known today) managed to form congregations and worship God without a bishop residing in the colonies until after the American Revolution.

The colonial denominations were nothing more than a loose network of congregations. If and when various communions developed structures of governance, their primary purposes were the ordination of ministers, the resolution of conflicts, and the support of new and existing congregations. Notably absent was any significant activity that could be described as mission. The denomination was only an embryo.

During the late eighteenth and early nineteenth centuries, the denomination as an organization was born. Inspiring this institutional change was the idea of mission — forged by the fires of evangelicalism and pietism which were reshaping Protestantism in the Western world. The church, it was argued, not only had a nature (right doctrine, correct worship); it also had a mission — the conversion of those outside the church, both enslaved and free; the

evangelization of people in other lands; the nurture and education
of people in the Christian faith and in all aspects of human knowledge; and the reform of society through an astonishing variety of
goals and means. Though the organizations differed in significant
ways, most Protestants adopted some organizational structure to
carry out denominational mission.[4]

How to organize a denomination for mission became a complex and difficult question in the early days of the American republic. The first impulse was to create organizations independent of
church structures and designed for special purposes. In the early
nineteenth century they were known as benevolent societies; today
they are often called para-church groups. Their causes ranged from
foreign missions (the American Board of Commissioners for Foreign Missions) and opposition to slavery (the American Anti-Slavery
Society) to issues that now seem amusing and quaint (The New
York Society for Providing Trusses to the Ruptured Poor).[5]

Since the nineteenth century, American Protestants have had
a love/hate relationship with these mission organizations which
operated alongside the denominations. While they initially encouraged members and congregations to support the benevolent
societies, the denominations eventually rose up and formed their
own ways of carrying out the mandates of mission and reform. The
benevolent societies died or were subsumed into denominations.
Of all the major benevolent societies of the early nineteenth century,
the only independent organization that survived into the late twentieth century was the American Bible Society. Other benevolent
societies eventually replaced the earlier organizations, but the
nineteenth century was the day of triumph for denominations as
missionary organizations.

The financing of denominations posed a new challenge for
American Protestants. Because they could no longer rely upon
public tax revenues, they developed a new and revolutionary means
of supporting the church — the freewill offering. Since the
nineteenth century, denominations have depended solely on the
willingness of their members to contribute money for their liveli-
hood and mission. Nineteenth-century evangelicals believed in
Arminianism, or the freedom of the will. Although there were
different interpretations of Arminianism, the doctrine had an or-

ganizational and economic parallel in the freewill offering. Church members voluntarily decided both whether to give and how much to give. This new development in financing religious institutions was an early sign of one of American society's unique characteristics — charitable giving through the private sector.[6]

Of course, nineteenth-century denominations differed in both polity and doctrine. Methodists and Episcopalians endorsed the office of bishop, while Baptists and Congregationalists abhorred it. Presbyterians lodged doctrinal authority in the Westminster Confession, while Disciples of Christ declared, "No creed but the Bible." Presbyterians, Congregationalists, and Baptists rejected the idea of forms for worship, while Episcopalians relied upon the liturgies of *The Book of Common Prayer*.

Amidst these differences was the idea of mission — the unifying theme in "the evangelical united front" of nineteenth-century American Protestantism. A denomination was not a church unless it engaged in mission, both at home and abroad. The purpose of mission was both the converting of "the heathen" and the spreading of the benefits of Western civilization. American Protestant missions included not only evangelism but also extensive educational efforts (the founding of schools, colleges, universities, and seminaries), medical work, and social and political reform. Americans were joined in the nineteenth-century missionary movement by European Protestants and by Roman Catholics. According to Kenneth Scott Latourette, the 1800s were "the Great Century" of Christian expansion.[7]

Thousands of men and women went to countries and colonies throughout the world. Thousands more served as missionaries to African Americans, Native Americans, members of other racial-ethnic minority groups, and people on the American frontier. Those who could not go as missionaries were constantly encouraged to support missions, and in many denominations, women were the primary source for financing foreign missions. For example, in the 1880s women of the Presbyterian Church in the U.S.A. (the northern branch of Presbyterianism) gave more money for missions than all of the other Presbyterian congregations combined. Restricted from holding church office in their own denominations, women eventually dominated the missionary movement outside the U.S.

By the end of the nineteenth century, the majority of Protestant missionaries were women.[8]

The Protestant idea of mission was rooted in two basic convictions: the absolute truth of Christianity and the moral superiority of Western culture. In 1897, the Congregationalist missionary Stanley L. Gulick declared, "Christianity is the religion of the dominant nations of the earth. Nor is it rash to prophesy that in due time it will be the only religion in the world." He explained the triumph of Christianity in these terms: "God means that the type of religion and civilisation attained by the Anglo-Saxon race shall have, for the present at least, the predominating influence in moulding the civilisation of the world. And everything points to the growing predominance of the Christian religion and Christian civilisation."[9]

Missionaries argued at length about whether "civilizing" preceded "Christianizing," but they were confident that one inevitably involved the other. Being exposed to other religions and other cultures, however, prompted them to be self-critical and raised new questions. The nineteenth-century missionary leader, Rufus Anderson, called for the new churches to become self-supporting, self-governing, and self-propagating as quickly as possible. By the early twentieth century, leaders of American mainstream Protestant missions had adopted much of Anderson's approach.[10]

If nineteenth-century denominations were institutions organized for mission, the truth is that they were not very well organized at all. Some channeled their funds and personnel through missionary organizations outside the denomination, such as the American Board of Commissioners for Foreign Missions. But the predominant pattern was denominational missions — boards and agencies that coordinated the missionary effort for a particular church. The result within each denomination and among denominations was enormous duplication of effort and intense competition for money, projects, and territory. Missions thrived in the marketplace of nineteenth-century Protestantism, but it was not an orderly market.[11]

The glue that held evangelical Protestant denominations together during the nineteenth century consisted of a common affirmation of the Bible's authority, the importance of committing one's life to Jesus Christ, and the mission to the world in word and deed.

Since there were so many options for expressing that mission, internal divisions within the denominations were minimized. Evangelical Protestants basically accepted their denominations as "constitutional confederacies," associations of congregations connected by relatively weak church structures and a broadly defined constitution.[12]

The Age of Incorporation

In the early twentieth century, mainstream Protestants developed a new organization for the denomination, modeled after the corporation. This "corporate denomination" has been the dominant way of understanding the organization of mainstream Protestant churches in the twentieth century. Like its counterpart in the economic realm, corporate denominations achieved great power and influence in the first part of the century, and by the end of the twentieth century they were significantly weakened.[13]

The corporate denomination appeared later than corporations in the world of business, but the impulse was the same. It was guided by a "search for order" in economics, politics, education, and other areas of American culture, including religion. The corporate denomination sought to reduce the duplication and competition in the missionary movement, and to bring order and efficiency to denominational life. Even though mainstream Protestants have used the corporate model in different ways, it prevailed as the new structure of denominational life.[14]

The corporate denomination is a complex institution. It is a bureaucratic, hierarchical organization, administered by managers with clear definitions of responsibility and authority. The corporate denomination has highly visible leaders, who can articulate a consensus about the mission of the denomination. Congregations support corporate denominations in exchange for goods and services (e.g., curriculum materials and assistance in finding ministers), and the denomination carries out mission in behalf of the congregations. What makes the corporate denomination effective is trust between congregations and the administrative structure, as well as between leaders and the denomination's constituency.[15]

The spirit of incorporation moved through all levels of the denominations, including the congregations. Ministers increasingly found their responsibilities expanded beyond preaching and pastoral care to the supervision of congregational employees — secretaries, sextons, etc. — and the administration of buildings and budgets. Even language changed in striking ways. People continued to refer to "the pastor's study," but increasingly it became known as "the pastor's office" where "the business" of the congregation was conducted. Governing boards of congregations began to act like boards of directors. Sunday schools developed their own hierarchies and bureaucracies with "superintendents" to administer them. The standardization of church school materials, such as the Uniform Bible Lessons, brought new order, predictability, and uniformity to the diversity of the Sunday school.[16]

The organizing of the American Baptist Convention in 1907 is a remarkable case study of the incorporation of American denominations, especially in a tradition that stressed the independence of congregations. During the nineteenth century, Northern Baptists conducted their mission through eight national societies formed between 1814 and 1891. Each was completely independent of the others, and each had its own board, budget, financial campaign, mailing list, and missionaries. During the 1890s, however, Baptists initiated efforts to reduce the competition and duplication of such efforts.

Behind the desire to create a unified structure for Baptist witness was the recognition that society had changed. No longer could independent congregations view mission as the conversion of individuals, whether at home or abroad. Shailer Mathews, a Northern Baptist and leader of the Social Gospel movement, declared, "The Christian spirit must be institutionalized if it is to prevail in the age of institutions."[17]

At the first meeting of the American Baptist Convention in 1907, delegates adopted three purposes for their new corporate denomination. "The object of this Convention," they declared, "shall be to give expression to the sentiment of its constituency upon matters of denominational importance and of general religious and moral interest; to develop denominational unity; and to give increased efficiency to efforts for the evangelization of America and the world." In an age of incorporation, efficiency became the litmus test of the corporate denomination. Baptists adopted efficiency as a standard and identified it with the early Christian church. "The test which the apostolic church . . . applied to its various operations, whether in its own organization or discipline, or in the extension of its administrative power, was its efficiency in accomplishing the mission for which the church itself was called into being. It is this idea which has been historically the fundamental principle of Baptist polity."[18]

Efficiency accomplished by trusted, visible leaders who administered mission programs endorsed by congregations — this was the hallmark of the corporate denomination in the first half of the twentieth century. Congregations supported national and international denominational efforts. Church publishing houses flourished, and denominational magazines were widely read. In the 1950s, *Presbyterian Life* pioneered the selling of block subscriptions to congregations, and its circulation exceeded 400,000 copies, making it the most widely circulated religious magazine in the U.S. The corporate denomination also made ecumenical cooperation feasible and more effective, and church finances were effectively administered.[19]

But even as it triumphed, forces were building that eroded the power and the authority of the corporate denomination.

The Denominational Revolution

The corporate denomination worked remarkably well during the first half of the twentieth century. However, debates over theology, mission, and power challenged and transformed the corporate denomination during the mid-twentieth century. These tensions are inextricably connected with one another, as well as with the crosscurrents within Christianity and the modern world. In each case, what mainstream Protestants confronted was the fragmentation of the corporate denomination. Its denominational identity was blurred by the rise of theological pluralism. The coherence of its mission was eroded by a contentious debate over mission priorities. Its institutional power declined as congregations increasingly asserted their autonomy and their own priorities.[20]

The debate over foreign missions was an early signal of how theological divisions would finally affect mainstream Protestant denominations as organizations. In 1932, the Laymen's Foreign Missions Inquiry issued its report, *Re-Thinking Missions,* by William Ernest Hocking. It prompted vehement protest from mainstream Protestant mission boards and their leaders. Hocking and his associates, who focused their inquiry primarily among some Asian missions, concluded that most of the mission enterprises were staffed by mediocre personnel, and boards should seek better qualified missionaries. But the Hocking Report, as it was called, was most controversial in advocating a theological shift toward modernism. Christian missions, it argued, should seek to respect and understand other cultures and religions. Missionaries should be ambassadors for Christ providing service, rather than witnesses for Christ seeking conversions.[21]

Prominent writer Pearl Buck, a daughter of the China mission, lauded the proposals of the Hocking Report, but most mission boards strongly resisted its conclusions. In addition, few active missionaries saw any value in such re-thinking. The report, however, reflected patterns of thought that had been circulating since the late nineteenth century — a growing awareness of other religions, the insights of biblical criticism and the new social sciences, and above all the "modernist impulse" to adapt Christian doctrine to new social realities. The nineteenth-century theology of missions — based on the absolute truth of Christianity and the superiority of Western culture — was gradually receding in mainstream Protestantism. A new theology of missions, sensitive to other cultures and religions, slowly emerged.[22]

Particularly after World War II, mainstream Protestant missions adopted a more ecumenical strategy with other American and European churches. The post-war period also brought the dismantling of the nineteenth-century colonial empires. With the rise of independent states came the ecclesiastical declaration of independence from Western Christian churches. The protest against the West and its missionary imperialism became so vehement that some church leaders in the 1960s called for "a moratorium on missions." *Missionary Go Home* (1964) epitomized this call to end world missions dominated by European and American Christians.[23]

American mainstream Protestants listened. Since then, their

missionary strategy has emphasized partnership with churches around the world, rather than superiority. Missionaries frequently bring some special skill or service, rather than a call to conversion. Fewer missionaries are "sent," and some are "received" from churches outside the United States.

The financing of American mainstream Protestant missions received a severe blow from the Great Depression of the 1930s. Moreover, theological changes made it difficult to justify the high levels of missionary activity of the nineteenth century. Henry P. Van Dusen, president of Union Seminary in New York and widely regarded as an influential representative of mainstream Protestantism, always affirmed his faith in the missionary enterprise. Yet he admitted in 1940 that "beneath all other misgivings was the basic query whether Christians were justified in striving to loose other peoples from ancient . . . loyalties in order to induct them into a strange and foreign faith."[24]

After World War II, the civil rights movement also challenged American mainstream Protestants to confront the ambiguous legacy of their missionary work with racial-ethnic minorities in American culture. African Americans, Asian Americans, Hispanic Americans, and Native Americans asserted in varying ways their protest against the racism and paternalism of white American mainstream Protestant missionary work among their people. At the same time, they celebrated the unique ways in which they had found religious and cultural identity as Christians. As minorities within the largely white denominations of mainstream Protestantism, they sought to secure their own place within its life and power structures. Yet they resisted assimilation within those structures and protested against the tendency to blur major differences within and among their diverse ethnic and cultural backgrounds.[25]

For example, Asian American Christians in these denominations included a wide variety of Asian backgrounds — Korean, Japanese, Taiwanese, and others. Similarly, Hispanic American Christians included those from Puerto Rico, Mexico, and Central and Latin America. The same pattern of cultural and religious differences existed among the African American and Native American communities within mainstream Protestantism. Invariably, each developed its own "caucus" or interest group, and they often banded together to lobby for funds and power within each mainstream Protestant denomination.[26]

Since World War II, mainstream Protestants and racial-ethnic minorities found themselves vacillating between two alternatives: independence for the minority groups (separate structures of power) or full integration into the structures of the denomination. The option of independence easily became the pattern of segregation, which had scarred the history of these denominations and American culture. The option of integration posed the danger of each group losing its distinctive identity and destroying the power and cohesion they had worked so hard to achieve.[27]

A comparable pattern of assimilation versus independence can be seen in the case of women and women's organizations within mainstream Protestantism. Congregationalists were the first to ordain women as ministers during the nineteenth century; the other mainstream Protestants did not accept women into the ordained ministry until after World War II. Women's organizations wielded enormous economic power within these denominations, especially in support of missionary efforts. They also comprised more than half of the membership within each denomination. Throughout the twentieth century, these women's organizations were sometimes independent of denominational structures and sometimes subsumed under denominational control.[28]

Neither option — assimilation or independence — gave women the power which their numbers and finances warranted. Like racial-ethnic minorities, women remained outsiders in the power structures of mainstream Protestant denominations.

During the 1960s, the legitimacy of power within the corporate denominations of mainstream Protestantism came under severe and withering criticism. Nearly all denominational leaders were white males, and pastors or priests and lay male leaders from large churches determined church policies. The background for the assault on the structures had been provided by decades of internal critique of the church as an institution. The assault coincided with the anti-institutionalism of the sixties, a deep questioning of the legitimacy of virtually all institutions in American culture — government, corporations, universities, schools, and churches.[29]

A struggle for political power broke out in these denominations. During the late sixties and early seventies, mainstream Protestants reorganized the corporate denomination in very significant ways. The influence of large churches and their male pastors or priests was drastically reduced; in succeeding decades, the so-called "tall steeple preachers" had difficulty gaining a hearing in denominational circles, ranging from the local to the national level. In their place arose the new voices searching for influence — small churches, racial ethnic minorities, women, and special interest groups.

The highly visible leaders of the corporate denomination were replaced with administrators who saw their primary task as managing the denomination's mission. The post-sixties leaders of mainstream Protestantism tended to have less pastoral experience and more background in church administration. They were responsive to liberal movements in theology and politics; they spread their beliefs in hiring like-minded associates. The structures created since the 1960s have accented inclusive access to power, consultation in decision making, and diffusion of authority and responsibility. These structures became umbrella organizations, in which largely invisible leaders pursued agendas of mission defined by themselves or by influential interest groups.[30]

The administrative leaders of the new denominational structures were idealists, seeking the reform of the church and the world. They were also politically astute, knowing how to seize the effective levers of power within the denominations. Their "new agenda" of social and corporate witness was an elaboration of theological ethics and social criticism in mainstream Protestantism throughout the twentieth century. It focused especially on race, war, feminism, and economic justice. The "new agenda" was needed in denominations whose complicity in the injustices of American society was legion. But the "new agenda" neglected major concerns of the "old agenda," especially relating to families, and it stood in tension with the priorities and values of many congregations and their members.[31]

Since the 1960s the managerial denomination has confronted two major problems. The first is a tendency to define the national agendas of denominations in tension or in conflict with the concerns of congregations. Because of their political skill and power, the

managers of mainstream Protestant denominations have been largely successful in changing policies, programs, and priorities. The new
emphases, however, have not been endorsed by congregations. The
result, according to William Fogleman and Louis Weeks, is denominations composed of two churches — the congregational church
and the governing body church, each with its own constituency
and agenda.[32] Looking back from the 1990s, one veteran church
administrator acknowledged the change in language drawn from
the Vietnam War: "We staged a *coup d'etat,* but we forgot to win
the hearts and minds of the people."

A second problem for the managerial denomination was the
fragmentation of mission itself. The corporate denomination
thrived on a relatively simple conception of mission for its identity
— national and international missions, Christian education, and
publications. Leaders knew what the church's mission should be
and could define and defend it. Congregations supported it. But
when the new denominational leaders criticized the nature of that
mission for its moral viability, few theological or ecclesiastical arguments were made for carrying out some forms of mission and not
others.

Mission multiplied, and the causes proliferated — from the
congregation to regional and national denominational agencies.
Church administrators were overwhelmed by the calls for the
church to be more involved in worthy efforts defended by committed groups. As mission fragmented, the managerial denomination behaved like a "regulatory agency," according to Craig Dykstra
and James Hudnut-Beumler. The image is unflattering but appropriate for describing the problem of power in managerial denominations. When there is little consensus about denominational priorities, denominational administrators find themselves trying to
manage and regulate the mission of the church.[33]

Both problems — fragmentation of mission and administrative
regulation — encouraged denominations to rely upon legislation,
rather than education, to determine the mission of a denomination.
Following the 1960s, the definition of a denomination subtly
shifted from a missionary organization to an organization managing
mission.

In politics and in church life, the structures of power in

American culture seemed increasingly legalistic, coercive, and intrusive. Mainstream Protestants wondered why their denominations had diminished in power, authority, and effectiveness. The answer lay in the dynamics of the organizational revolution which has transformed virtually every institution in American society.

Money for Mission: The Untold Story

The debate about mission and the struggle to broaden power in mainstream Protestant denominations involved critical theological issues, as well as basic values about Christian discipleship. This debate and struggle obscure a longer-term change in the financing of the church — a change that has enormous consequences for these denominations and American church life as a whole.

At the outset, it has to be acknowledged that we know relatively little about the economic history of churches in American culture. The subject has received scant attention, and the research that we do have usually focuses on the recent past. What is clearly needed is more research over long periods of time, that determines how and why people support churches and other religious institutions and how they allocate their money.

One study of the Presbyterian Church in the U.S. and the Reformed Church in America since the mid-nineteenth century tells the following story. Congregations provided the cash that financed denominational mission as well as the expansion of the corporate denomination in the twentieth century. Despite the devastating impact of the Great Depression, congregations remained constant in their support of denominational mission, spending approximately $2 on themselves (ministerial salaries, utilities, etc.) for every $1 spent on denominational mission.[34]

Congregations remained constant, that is, until the 1950s. During the early 1950s mainstream Protestant congregations increased their giving but steadily allocated more funds for their own use. Their consumption of charitable dollars increased steadily throughout the next decades; by the 1990s, congregations were spending $8 or $9 on their own needs for every $1 they sent to the national denominational structures.[35]

The shift in allocating funds was extraordinary and revolutionary, breaking the pattern of more than a century of economic behavior. Why did this revolutionary change occur? Obviously, the shift began at the height of the corporate denomination's influence — even before there was significant conflict over mission priorities or social and political issues.

The answer to why the economic shift occurred lies in the transformation of congregational life, wrought in part by the baby boom. The huge increase in children coming to church, the need for more programs for them and their parents, and the demands for more specialized ministries — in short, the religious revival of the 1950s — launched a dramatic and far-reaching change in how congregations allocated their funds. Church members continued to give more, but their congregations needed more and consumed the increase.[36]

Since the 1960s, denominational conflict over social, political, and theological issues may have exacerbated this trend, especially the tendency to designate money for particular causes both inside and outside the denominations. Localism — the desire to spend money on clearly identifiable causes at the local level — was another critical factor. For example, in 1989 Presbyterians contributed a total of $1.8 billion to their churches. Approximately $1.3 billion was spent for "local programs" (ministerial salaries and congregational support) and local mission projects. While national denominational support totalled $47.7 million, designated giving for Presbyterian and non-Presbyterian causes totalled $61.8 million.[37]

The trend toward designation and local giving, perhaps ironically, was partially encouraged by the denominations themselves. Since the 1970s, mainstream Protestant denominations have encouraged congregations to support more forms of mission, and to do so with only the lowest practical levels of denominational structures.[38]

Under pressure from their own members, mainstream Protestant congregations gradually transformed the corporate denomination. Congregations bought the personnel, services, and the physical plant they needed for ministry. When conflict over national programs developed, congregations increasingly designated their finances for local purposes or for causes they chose and approved.

Faced with the shift of finances, the new managerial denomination attempted to encourage congregational initiatives while struggling to maintain the external structures of the corporate denomination.

The New Denomination

By the 1990s, the outline of the denominational revolution was clear. Congregations, rather than denominations, had become the primary mission organizations in American mainstream Protestantism.

The denominational revolution is not over, and its full implications are not yet evident. A large part of the alienation and conflict in mainstream Protestant denominations arises out of the confusion generated by these dramatic changes, as well as out of the difficulty in assessing what these changes mean for the future.

Some signs of the new shape of mainstream Protestant denominations are fairly obvious. Their mission is now more broadly defined and is being carried out through a wide variety of organizations, not simply through the denominations themselves. As noted earlier, mainstream Protestant denominations have been very ambivalent about para-church organizations; the corporate denomination — for both theological and institutional reasons — resisted their incursion. As mainstream Protestants changed their theological emphases and adjusted their mission priorities in the twentieth century, para-church groups once again moved into the breach.

For example, in foreign missionary activity in the early 1920s there were some 14,000 North American Protestant missionaries, the vast majority of whom were denominationally supported. By the mid-1980s the number of North American Protestant missionaries exceeded 39,000; 90 percent of them were funded through non-denominational mission organizations.[39] By the late 1980s, The Evangelical Alliance Mission (TEAM), a non-denominational missionary organization, had more career missionaries in the field than the Presbyterians and United Methodists combined.[40]

Similarly, as mainstream Protestants reconsidered their commitment to youth ministries, Young Life was launched in 1941 — partly by Presbyterian leaders. By 1988, it had a budget of $38

million, which was nearly 40 percent of the entire General Assembly
budget of the Presbyterian Church (USA). A similar story can be
told about the displacement of mainstream Protestant campus ministries and the rise of Inter-Varsity after 1939 and Campus Crusade
after 1951. But perhaps the most dramatic story of evangelical
Protestant expansion of mission is World Vision, established in
1950. By the mid-1990s, it had become the second largest Christian
organization for international relief. Its budget surpassed Church
World Service, supported primarily by mainstream Protestants; only
Caritas, the Roman Catholic international relief organization, is
larger.[41]

Para-church groups enjoy the appeal of a specialized ministry,
as opposed to the multifaceted ministries of denominations. Local
mission projects — the rescue mission, the home for battered
women and children, a literacy project — likewise benefit. The
multifaceted and variegated mission of a denomination suffers by
comparison.

In short, in the kaleidoscope of American religious institutions,
denominations and para-church groups trade mission emphases
back and forth. Mission — in all of its variety — continues. What
denominations do not accomplish often becomes fertile ground for
new organizations and specialized ministries. Whether Christian
mission itself suffers is unclear. But because of the denominational
revolution, the mission of denominations and para-church groups
in the late twentieth century has changed the landscape of American
and world Christianity.

Today mainstream Protestant denominations confront the reality of no longer dominating American culture. Other churches
have far larger memberships. Among mainstream Protestants, there
is more switching than ever before. Therefore, when sociologists
talk about the declining significance of denominationalism for mainstream Protestantism, they are right in two ways. These denominations have become smaller than they once were, and they have
become less powerful in preserving the allegiance of their members.

But the denominational revolution and the declining significance of denominationalism does not mean that denominations are
going to die. In a society of disestablished churches, if denominations did not exist, they would have to be invented. This chapter

has demonstrated that the definition of a denomination has changed dramatically and often in American history. Being a Methodist in 1790 was very different from being a Methodist in 1990. One lesson of denominational history is that denominations have an uncanny ability to improvise, change, and adapt. In fact, amidst all the appearance of ecclesiastical gridlock, denominations may be among the most creative organizations in American culture in responding to social change.

Some of these creative adaptations of denominational structures are already emerging. Several middle-governing bodies (presbyteries, conferences, dioceses) are experimenting with new programs designed to support congregations and build cooperation between parishes. Some denominations are utilizing technology, such as electronic mail and video, to accelerate communication between denominational structures and congregations. Several denominations recognize the importance of developing informal networks of individuals and congregations to develop programs or to support mission causes, such as world hunger or youth ministries. An emphasis on hierarchy and the right process of decision making has slowly given way to the empowerment of individuals and congregations for achieving common goals.

According to Nancy Ammerman, the emerging denomination recognizes the variety of needs and aspirations of its congregations. By working through coalitions and networks and by assuming the gifts and skills of its constituency, the denomination can respond to its diverse membership. Denominations do have a future after all.[42]

The challenge before the emerging denomination is to forge a compelling theological vision and sufficiently flexible organizational structures — those that will allow the creativity of the congregations to flourish in communion with other congregations, rather than to languish alone. After decades of being attacked for their vices and even their existence, mainstream Protestant denominations still retain enormous material and religious resources for living out the gospel in the twenty-first century.

6. *An Open Letter to Mainstream Protestants*

Brothers and Sisters in Christ:

We have debated how to end this book. In the midst of our writing, we ran into a pastor of a small urban church in the North-east. Her congregation is typical of many mainstream Protestant congregations. During the 1950s its membership was more than 800; by the 1990s it had dwindled to approximately 175.

When we told her we were writing about what had happened in mainstream Protestantism in the twentieth century, she asked, "Will it be a hopeful book?"

That question helped crystalize what this last chapter has become. We realize that the portrait of mainstream Protestantism painted in previous chapter includes many dark hues and shadows. Nonetheless, producing a "hopeful book" simply to lift the spirits of this community of Christians would be a disservice to their church and to the Christ they seek to serve. But we do see vital signs in mainstream Protestantism — both in what it is and what it can do.[1] It is these prospects for a vibrant future witness that we wish to address in this letter.

We think this sometimes beleaguered band of denominations has a distinctive Christian witness and can contribute both to American society and to the world. The three of us are mainstream Protestants, both by birth and by conviction. We were baptized, confirmed, and ordained as Presbyterians. We know this makes us unusual; in our own denomination, 59 percent of present members were reared in another church.[2]

We are mainstream Protestants primarily because of our beliefs. We believe with other mainstream Protestants that our hope and our strength are rooted in the fact that Jesus Christ is Lord, and that through him we are offered new life and forgiveness from sin. We believe that God created the world and pronounced it good, but that human life is a mixed sphere where intractable evil and potential goodness struggle constantly for ascendancy. We believe that God has called forth the church in its many forms to witness to the power of God's love in Jesus Christ, a sacrificial love that assures the eventual triumph of God.

We acknowledge the pluralism of belief in our world, and yet we affirm the gospel as "the power of God for salvation to everyone who has faith" (Rom. 1:16). We recognize multiple signs of decline in the mainstream Protestant situation, but we see life signs that indicate the unfolding of God's reign on this earth and beyond. This letter, therefore, is a modest attempt to fulfill the injunction in 1 Peter: "Always be ready to make your defense to anyone who demands from you an accounting for the hope that is in you; yet do it with gentleness and reverence" (1 Peter 3:15).

Listen to the leading of the Holy Spirit.

This book makes clear the magnitude of change that American mainstream Protestant churches have experienced in the twentieth century. We have emphasized how deeply these developments have affected the life and mission of mainstream Protestant denominations, and have shown that the world in which they must minister is a new world. We will not soften our insistence that the churches confront these new realities, but we also recognize that these changes frequently seem baffling and overwhelming.

The most powerful factors shaping our churches have been those that have transformed American society as a whole. The religious and cultural disestablishment of mainstream Protestantism is the long-term consequence of the separation of church and state and the growing diversity of American culture. Changing demographics — especially the demographics of the baby boomers — explains a great deal about membership growth and decline. Greater emphasis on choice and more freedom to exercise choices made switching a prevalent pattern in American religious life. The denominational revolution was fueled by congregations demanding more ministry to themselves and their communities.

For each change in our churches there was usually a parallel pattern in some other part of American society. For example, during the coffee hour at church, a friend remarked, "I've been thinking about you and your research this week." He is a business executive with the *Courier-Journal* newspaper in Louisville. He continued, "I've been at a journalism conference, and one of the main issues was how newspapers can attract and retain readers when there's no 'brand loyalty' any more. That's a lot like the problem of denominations today."

This friend was right. His insight helps put the transformation of mainstream Protestantism in perspective. Our challenges rise out of the broader movements and difficult dilemmas facing nearly every institution in our culture.

In the midst of these changes, however, we are convinced that the Holy Spirit is creating something new in American mainstream Protestantism and in the Christian church. A central task of the church at this time is to listen and respond to the leading of the Spirit, rather than becoming paralyzed and passive. Those elements that appear to be threats may be God's call to new and deeper forms of discipleship.

➤ *Vital Sign: An Opportunity for Awakening*

Strange as it may seem in our current situation, extensive social change, such as we are now confronting, has been in the past a vital sign of an old American Protestant opportunity — "an awakening." The term was first used in the nineteenth century to describe the outpouring of religious enthusiasm and conversions that appeared in the mid-1700s. That outpouring became known as the First Great Awakening. A subsequent revival during the late 1700s and early 1800s became the Second Great Awakening. The

term was always applied by church leaders to describe a period of
religious renewal.

   Careful historical analysis has demonstrated that these awakenings involved far more than the conversion of individuals to
Christianity and the expansion of church membership. It is now
clear that both awakenings were part of a process of massive social
change. For example, the First Great Awakening helped shape the
values and ideas that contributed to the American Revolution.[3] The
Second Great Awakening helped forge the values and institutions
of the early Republic.[4]

   The historian William McLoughlin has used the idea of awakenings as a metaphor for describing critical transitions in American
religious history.[5] Using the anthropological work of Anthony F. C.
Wallace, McLoughlin argues that an awakening is a period in which
the basic values of a culture are redefined. Such an awakening always
involves intense conflict over social, political, economic, and moral
issues, pitting agents of change against agents of preservation. An
awakening ends, he says, with a revitalization of culture and a revival
of those religious communities that are able to draw on elements
of their traditions in new ways to address the culture's changing
understanding of itself and the world. Prior definitions of morality,
the good society, and the church are never completely rejected, but
they are reconceived.

   Interestingly, McLoughlin, who published his work in 1978,
proposed that American society was in an "awakening" which
began in 1960 and might end in the 1990s. At the heart of the
"awakening" was the crucible of moral issues with which mainstream Protestants have been struggling — race, war, class, gender,
sexuality, and the disproportionate political and economic power
of the United States.

   We recognize that it seems hard to imagine the turmoil of the
past several decades as an "awakening." Although the term is only
a metaphor, clearly our understanding of the Christian life has been
transformed. Mainstream Protestants are no longer willing to accept
a segregated society based on the idea that God has ordained white
people as superior to black people. We reject the anti-Catholicism
and anti-Semitism that have scarred our past. Most of us refuse to
equate American military policy with God's providence. We know

that poverty does not symbolize the moral failure of the poor. The equality of women is accepted as never before. Most of our denominations have adopted policies that affirm that gay and lesbian people should not suffer economic or political discrimination. Despite all of its positive effects, we know that our political and economic power has severely damaged the environment.

Few mainstream Protestants would have been willing to make those religious and ethical judgments a century ago. A moral and religious "awakening" has transformed mainstream Protestantism. These deeper insights into the richness of the Christian faith and the complexity of human life are certainly a vital sign of a faithful Christian community.

➤ *Vital Sign: Engaging a Changing Culture*

We mainstream Protestants cannot control or determine the moral values of this nation or any other nation. Nevertheless, during this century we have become faithful to a central feature of our heritage — a willingness to engage the changing culture of our era. We have refused to ignore the great issues of our age, however imperfectly we have responded to them.

This persistent and courageous engagement with our culture is one very important vital sign of our life as God's people. But it will lead to a revivified church only if we resist two impulses that have distorted our response to recent social change.

The first of these impulses has been what can be called the "Mars Hill syndrome" (Acts 17:16-34). In our willingness to be receptive to new ideas, mainstream Protestants too often look like the Athenians who listened to Paul on Mars Hill; that is, we sample religious ideas from every conceivable source. Obviously, new religious perspectives can enrich our understanding of the Christian faith, and we should never sacrifice the spirit of creative inquiry that has marked our tradition. Still, not everything that is novel is good or even worth taking seriously.

The second and more important impulse has been a tendency to see the Christian life in simplistic "either/or" terms. As noted in our introduction, part of the genius of mainstream Protestantism has been its attempt to maintain the tensions inherent in Christianity — grace and works, judgment and mercy, heart and mind, the individual and the community, and being "in but not of" this world. These conflicting allegiances represent the dilemma of discipleship. Each pole is a virtue, yet each becomes a true virtue only when held in tension with its counterpart.[6]

Unfortunately the twentieth century has seen too much of our inability to maintain those tensions — for example, insisting on the priority of deed evangelism over word evangelism, jettisoning new church development in favor of ministries of social justice, abandoning the "old agenda" of individual and family ethics for the "new agenda" of corporate and systemic ethics.

In our zeal to understand what is new, we should remember the value of the past. In our passion to reshape the church and the world, we should weigh the importance of what we may be laying aside. In sum, let us keep our heads; it is difficult to live through an "awakening." As we sort through the changes that have occurred and look to the future, we would do well to remember the words of the apostle Paul: "Do not be conformed to this world, but be transformed by the renewing of your minds, so that you may discern what is the will of God — what is good and acceptable and perfect" (Rom. 12:2).

Listening to the leading of the Holy Spirit involves that difficult task of discerning God's will, but our hope rests in the promise of God's enduring presence and the guidance of the Holy Spirit in every age. The mainstream Protestant tradition will always be tempted to embrace too much of the world or to retreat from its realities. Transformation by the renewing of our minds — listening to the Holy Spirit — is a key to our calling to be in but not of the world.

Live the faith.

The Gospels tell the story of a woman who had been suffering from hemorrhages for twelve years. "She had endured much under many physicians, and had spent all that she had; and she was no better, but rather grew worse." She heard about Jesus and resolved that if she could only touch the hem of his garment, she would be healed. Despite a crowd pressing around Jesus, she accomplished her mission. According to the Gospels, Jesus inquired, "Who touched my clothes?" Under the circumstances, it was a ludicrous question, and the disciples told him so. Eventually the woman came forward and confessed that she had touched his robe. Jesus declared, "Daughter, your faith has made you well; go in peace and be healed of your disease" (Mark 5:24-34; see also Matt. 9:18-26; Luke 8:40-56).

This story illustrates one of our primary conclusions about mainstream Protestants in the twentieth century. The crucial challenge for these churches is their faith. Like the hemorrhaging woman, mainstream Protestant churches have endured much from many physicians. At times, it seems they are not getting better from their afflictions but growing worse. Like the woman, they need to decide to get better, knowing they cannot heal themselves. They need to touch their Lord. They will discover that in reaching out in faith, God will make them well.

As indicated earlier, mainstream Protestants have been very adept at ignoring the magnitude of the changes sweeping across their churches and across American culture. This has been especially true regarding membership decline, where the level of denial is high because virtually every congregation has been affected.[7]

What if these congregations learned that their decline was due to a disease? Like so many illnesses, the disease is the result both of their own deeds and of influences beyond their control. For example, mainstream Protestant denominations did curtail their initiatives in new church development, but they had no control over the national birth rates. They can, however, decide to get better, and the key is their faith — a willingness to touch the garment of Jesus and to admit to it publicly. What will that new health look like?

➤ *Vital Sign: Dependence on the Word of God in Scripture*

At the core of Protestant faith is our dependence on the authority of Scripture. The Reformers united in affirming *sola Scriptura,*

"Scripture alone," as the source of knowledge of God and salvation through Jesus Christ. We have been known as "people of the book," and from this stance has come the extraordinary emphasis upon literacy and education in the Protestant tradition.

The authority of Scripture is perhaps the most contentious doctrine in contemporary Protestantism — for a variety of reasons. Critical scholarship has made it difficult to understand and interpret ancient texts in terms of modern ideas. Complex moral issues of today seem irresolvable by reference to specific biblical passages. We are certain that we reject the interpretations of fundamentalists, who insist on the inerrancy of Scripture, but many of us stutter in defining a clear and persuasive alternative understanding of the Bible's authority. Consequently, we read Scripture less frequently. As a result, the most devastating and debilitating characteristics of Protestant life today are widespread biblical illiteracy and the tendency to simply ignore Scripture as the authority for the Christian life.

Why have Protestants affirmed the Bible as authoritative? Because it is the source of our knowledge of God's salvation in Jesus Christ. Through the guidance of the Holy Spirit, the words of Scripture become God's Word to us. That Word is first and foremost a declaration of God's love — sacrificial, self-giving love that forgives our sins and unites us with God through the life, death, and resurrection of Jesus Christ. The Word, moreover, is a revelation of God's will for our lives.

The message of Scripture is salvation; the medium for its power is the Holy Spirit. John Calvin put it this way: "For as God alone is a fit witness of himself in his Word, so also the Word will not find acceptance in men's hearts before it is sealed by the inward testimony of the Spirit. . . . Hence, it is not right to subject [Scripture] to proof and reasoning. And the certainty it deserves with us, it attains by the testimony of the Spirit. For even if it wins reverence for itself by its own majesty, it seriously affects us only when it is sealed upon our hearts through the Spirit."[8]

Reading the Bible with the prayer that the Holy Spirit will speak God's Word to us is risky, for it involves confronting both God and ourselves in the light of God's intention for our lives. As Robert McAfee Brown has written, "This, it must be insisted, is the *real* reason we seek to dismiss the Bible: not because it is out-of date, but because it is much too up-to-date, because it describes far too accurately who we are and where we have gone wrong. It is not fanciful at all to talk about being 'participants' in the biblical story, for we are participants in that story whether we will or no — participants who are the objects both of the promises it puts before us and of the demands it no less urgently puts before us."[9]

One of the most important vital signs of a renewed Protestant witness will be our reliance on Scripture as the authority for our lives: the recognition that through these pages comes a truth that will set us free from ourselves and for others. One woman in a Louisville congregation put it this way: "What I'm looking for," she said, "is an authority that will not oppress me." As individuals and institutions, we need to decide that we want to be different — that we wish to be healed of the hemorrhaging of life and vitality and reach out for Christ's robe. The hem of that garment is the Word of God revealed in the Bible through the work of the Holy Spirit.

The authority of Scripture and its message of salvation are the necessary foundation for any kind of outreach we extend to others. Earlier we noted that two characteristics of growing churches are the decision to grow and openness to new people. Most people join congregations because they are invited. Animating the congregations those people join are a conviction that they want to grow and an ability to welcome new people. Behind the invitation to come to church is the members' belief that the church has a message that is both meaningful and challenging.

When we mainstream Protestants remember that faith is at the heart of the church and that the Bible is the source of our knowledge of what it means to live faithfully under God, then we will find new health. From that base of new vitality, mainstream Protestants will develop the evangelistic outreach needed for the new world in which we minister. The outlines of a faithful strategy for renewal and outreach, it seems to us, are now fairly clear.

The most obvious first steps will be to reach both lapsed members and racial-ethnic minorities.[10]

➤ *Vital Sign: The Challenge*
of the Inactive and Unaffiliated

Many lapsed members are "mental members." They identify themselves as Episcopalians or Methodists even though they do not
regularly attend any congregation. Their number is legion. For
example, after Presbyterians reunited in 1983, the new denomination commissioned a marketing firm to determine the kinds of
publications needed. After surveying a scientifically selected sample
of the American public, the firm reported that there were six million
Presbyterians in America. At that time, the new denomination had
on its rolls a membership of only a little more than three million.
Even if the other small Presbyterian denominations were included,
that would not account for the additional three million Americans
who claimed Presbyterian affiliation.[11]

Some of these inactive members are not just lapsed members
but unaffiliated, and most of these are baby boomers. Will they
return? They already are coming back to church, partly because
they are seeking what their parents sought — religious instruction
for their children. One key to attracting the baby boomers is to
develop programs for their children and for them as families.

The unaffiliated are also willing to return. One project sur-
veyed two samples of unchurched Americans and former Presbyterians, age 18 or older. The results were astonishing. Among the
general population, 61 percent said they were "very likely" or
"somewhat likely" to consider attending church more frequently.
Among former Presbyterians, the response was even more affirm-
ative: 82 percent declared they were "very likely" or "somewhat
likely" to resume regular participation.

The two samples responded almost identically to queries on
what they expected from congregations. Meaningful worship, especially good preaching, was mentioned by virtually all of them. "A
sermon that relates Bible teachings to today's problems" was cited
as very important or somewhat important by 96 percent of the
inactives in the American population and 97 percent of the Presbyterian inactives. Both samples prefer informal music in services,
and they want more flexible times to worship, such as Saturday
evening.

The inactive and unaffiliated are looking for congregations that offer a wide range of ministries to them and to their communities — programs for the hungry and the homeless, groups for the elderly, counseling programs, youth education and Bible study groups, nursery schools, programs for singles, and sports groups. They think the church should contribute to society, but they vehemently reject overt political involvement.

They also believe spirituality is very important, affirming that people need interaction with others to maintain their faith. But they think that the church as an institution is not very important. Like many even within the church, the unaffiliated are yearning for the spiritual and seeking relationships. They want to find God as well as a sense of life's meaning. They bond to people, not institutions.

Perhaps the most telling response was elicited by a question posed to the Presbyterian inactives: "If a good friend asked you to go along to church one Sunday, how likely would you be to go with your friend?" "Very likely" or "somewhat likely" was the answer given by 86 percent of the former Presbyterians.[12]

The lesson is clear. The unchurched are waiting to be invited. But we must take the first step and issue the invitation.

➤ *Vital Sign: The Contribution of Racial-Ethnic Minorities*

Reaching racial-ethnic minorities presents us with more complex challenges. Our legacy of ministry has been distorted by racism and paternalism. Our membership is overwhelmingly white. Our requirements for ordination and our styles of worship frequently conflict with the standards, values, and practices in African American, Asian American, and Hispanic American communities.

As we have seen, our churches have vacillated between a model of separate and often segregated structures for racial-ethnic minorities and a model of assimilation.[13] We believe strongly that the ideal of integration — in church and society — should not be abandoned. The church should be an inclusive body, rejecting the barriers of race and class. When churches capitulate to these divisions, they perpetuate the brokenness of the body of Christ.

Racial-ethnic congregations, however, represent a legitimate quest for community and meaning in a fragmented and often hostile society. We believe that an inclusive denomination can and should include a wide variety of congregations with the freedom and autonomy to express the Christian faith in their own unique ways.

A critical challenge for mainstream Protestants is whether we will be willing to support the formation of such congregations: Will we provide the freedom and financial support to strengthen and extend ministries? We have discovered that the missionary churches we have founded in other countries prosper and grow with our help and without our leadership. That lesson can now be brought back home.

It is very obvious that mainstream Protestantism must not rely on the white population as its membership base in the twenty-first century. That would be a grave mistake. Even more importantly, the vision of the body of Christ — so dramatically described by Paul in his letters and embodied in his ministry — makes the broadening of the church a spiritual mandate, rather than simply a practical necessity.

➤ *Vital Sign: The Development of New Congregations of Believers*

A related challenge before mainstream Protestants is the mission of new church development. In most cases, this task is greater than any one or a few congregations can accomplish alone. It demands the coordination and cooperation for which denominations are suited if they are flexible and inventive in their planting of congregations.

New church starts in mainstream Protestant denominations peaked during the 1950s. They then dropped dramatically in the late 1960s and the 1970s. More recently, the number of new church projects has risen above their previous lows, but they still do not approach the activity of the 1950s.[14]

This pattern stands in sharp contrast with two of the fastest growing denominations of this century, the Assemblies of God and the Southern Baptist Convention. New church development efforts in both denominations fell in number during roughly the same period as mainstream Protestant slippage occurred. But even at their lowest ebb, their new church starts exceeded that of mainstream Protestants, and in the late 1980s, Southern Baptist congregational plantings had almost returned to their 1950s highs, while the Assemblies of God had actually surpassed their 1950s performance.[15]

Recent research indicates that new church development patterns in the latter two denominations were both *cause* and *symptom* of their consistently vigorous membership outreach in the last forty-five years. Put another way, new church starts do not completely account for their membership expansion during this century, but such projects certainly contributed to it.[16]

The same research suggests, however, that new church development has had an even more direct causal relationship with mainstream Protestant church growth, or the lack thereof. As Penny Marler and Kirk Hadaway put it, "When these denominations make the effort to start new churches, they tend to grow (or at least moderate their declines). When they do not make the effort, they tend to decline."[17]

This is as it should be since the new births of congregations in the family of God are like new births in the human family. They are, at their best, a sign and symbol of love shared, a love, in the church's case, enjoyed together by fellow disciples in Christ that yearns to be shared beyond its present congregational confines with new congregants of people from different locales, generations, and cultures.

➤ *Vital Sign: Campus Ministry*
  as a Mission Field

College and university campuses are a neglected area of mission in American culture today. Their atmosphere is overwhelmingly secular; the curricula often ignore religion and religious institutions, and on occasion are openly hostile to religious practice. We are convinced that the evangelism strategy for mainstream Protestants should include a renewed focus on campus ministry.[18]

Studies show that mainstream Protestants have difficulty retaining their young. The ritual of leaving home is frequently a ritual of leaving the church as well. Mainstream Protestantism's absence in higher education will only perpetuate the linking of these two rituals.[19]

If we are going to forge new ministries in higher education, two actions must be taken. First, mainstream Protestant campus ministry should be reconceived as evangelism. Its prevailing models were developed for established churches who assumed that higher education would reinforce Christian belief and values. That has obviously changed. We think churches should recognize this new environment and see the primary purpose of campus ministry to be an informed and persuasive presentation of Christianity, as well as an invitation to join the Christian community.

Second, mainstream Protestants will have to develop a variety of forms for campus ministry. In some cases, congregations near a campus will be a viable option. In other situations, ecumenical cooperation among mainstream Protestant denominations may be effective. But we also suggest that the ecumenical spectrum broaden itself and encourage cooperation with other Protestant groups on campus, such as Inter-Varsity. Mainstream Protestants have a long history of cooperating with, rather than competing against, the para-church groups of American Christianity. No single denomination or group of denominations will be able to penetrate the vast system of American higher education. We can and should find new friends and allies in our common mission.

➤ *Vital Sign: Social Service as Mission*

In their evangelism, mainstream Protestants should also recognize and strengthen the inherent altruism of Americans, especially the young. Social service programs are stirring within the new ecosystem of mainstream Protestant congregations, and this impulse can be nurtured and strengthened.

The church can wield tremendous power in our society by reminding people that they are not powerless; they can in fact make a difference with God's direction and power. What is critical, however, is that churches provide a specifically Christian framework to supply motivation and meaning to people's gift of time, energy, and money. Prayer, Bible study, worship, and discussion should be explicit and unapologetic features of the evangelism of service.

These strategies of outreach are suggestions for our churches. They are based on research as well as on the experiences of congregations. The strategies are not, however, cures for the maladies of mainstream Protestantism.

Healing comes by reaching out in faith, as the hemorrhaging woman discovered. The vital signs of mainstream Protestantism can be strengthened by people who likewise reach out in faith — in voice and through service.

Love the church.

In 1800, as "the Great Century" of Christian expansion was dawning, the Congregationalist Timothy Dwight composed the hymn "I Love Thy Kingdom, Lord." It included this verse:

> I love Thy Church, O God:
> Her walls before Thee stand,
> Dear as the apple of Thine eye,
> And graven on Thy hand.[20]

Nearly two centuries later, Dwight's words sound strange amidst the conflicts within mainstream Protestantism. National denominational meetings, intending to embody the unity of these churches, often reveal the deep divisions within their fellowships. These divisions may be rooted in the contending parties' love for the church, but their language and tactics disguise their love for one another — the same love that Christ commissioned the church to embody. Indeed, one volume of Martin E. Marty's survey of religion in the twentieth century is subtitled simply "The Noise of Conflict."[21]

The sources of division are real and complex. Politics becomes divisive as groups struggle to maintain or obtain power over denominational programs and agencies. Since power in mainstream Protestant denominations is diffused, these battles are very complicated, ranging from the local to the national level. Like American politics generally, a key issue of the internal political debates in mainstream Protestantism has been representation — whose voices are heard, and who makes decisions. The issue of representation is especially controversial for two reasons. First, special interest groups often dominate the discussion because their organizational and political savvy amplify their voices. Second, denominations frequently resort to legislating representation by quotas. This encourages resentment because the church seems to act more like a regulatory agency than a community of mutual support.[22]

Denominational divisions are also rooted in theology and ethics. There are significant theological differences within our denominations, committed as they are to diversity of belief. Mainstream Protestants also disagree on major ethical issues in American society. These disagreements sometimes take the form of "culture wars" over a wide range of subjects, and most of them today are related to family, gender, and sexuality.[23]

Interestingly, research suggests that the phenomena of "culture wars" and theological pluralism are less prevalent *within* congregations, which internally tend to be more homogeneous in their attitudes and beliefs.[24] Instead, the battles are more often waged on denominational turf. Denominational structures have been severely weakened by the organizational revolution and the shift of power to the congregations. Denominations are therefore ill-equipped to deal with these struggles, and the debates themselves drain denominational energy and resources.

Validating the divisions within our denominations has been the theological legacy of self-criticism, often called "the Protestant principle."[25] This idea holds that since God alone is sovereign, all human constructions — institutions as well as doctrines — are finite and therefore subject to criticism. As one looks at the Protestant movement since the sixteenth century, it is clear that this principle has been invoked frequently and fervently. Conflict and disagreement about the nature of the church have been a staple of our history, not an exception.

Within mainstream Protestantism in the twentieth century, critiques of the church have escalated because of the internal civil war between liberals and conservatives. Neo-orthodoxy's negative assessment of denominationalism and the church's capitulation to "the American way of life" exposed the frailty of mainstream Protestant churches. Since the 1960s, the theological and social criticism of the church has escalated and broadened into a moral critique of Christianity itself.

These critics of the church were invariably idealistic reformers who implicitly and explicitly saw the organized church as a strong and viable institution. As we can now see, however, the religious and cultural disestablishment of mainstream Protestantism, the waning of the Protestant ecosystems of nurture, theological changes, and the organizational revolution within denominations — all of these discordant elements make the churches weaker than they once might have appeared. Coming amidst the growing distrust of all institutions in American culture, the critique of the church has created a pervasive crisis of confidence in mainstream Protestantism.

➤ *Vital Sign: The Denomination as Community*

The critique of the church must not end, but the time has come to change the context for debate. Our churches are much more fragile than we have acknowledged. Denominations are not perfect expressions of the body of Christ. But on the contemporary Christian landscape, the denomination is a visible vital sign of a central Christian conviction. Denominations seek to incarnate the divine commission to live life together.

Ideally, denominations should be communities of faith composed not only of comfortable and like-minded friends but also of aliens and strangers. Denominations seek to nurture and sustain faith and stewardship in a community larger than the pockets of homogeneity that congregations have become in our choice-driven culture. Despite their manifold failings to live out the full scope of Christian discipleship, denominations at their best strive to proclaim a gospel of God's love and compassion, and welcome the richness that diversity brings.

Although we disagree with the critics of the church on many significant theological and ethical issues, two particular disagreements are worth noting. First, the meaning of the word "Protestant" is only partially explored by conceiving these churches as self-critical. The legacy of Protestantism at its best has been much more than a protest against others' or its own finite and fallible understanding of the Christian faith. Second, the Protestant Reformers also protested *by professing* a new vision of Christianity — one that would build faith, commitment, confidence, and service to God. This professing that nurtures and undergirds the faith of a diverse community is as much a part of the Protestant tradition as its self-critical character. We would do well to recover this professing aspect of Protestantism during this time of internal conflict.

We should also note that mainstream Protestants may be closer to one another than we recognize. For example, the *Presbyterian Panel,* a regular poll of ministers, elders, and members in the Presbyterian Church (USA), reveals a bell-shaped curve on virtually every contested theological and social issue over the last several years. At the conservative and very liberal ends of the spectrum are small minorities — perhaps 10–15 percent. The remaining 70–80 percent find themselves within the bell curve. Because special interest groups of the right and the left tend to shape denominational discussions, the vast majority remains inarticulate.[26]

We need more voices that express what we share together rather than what divides us. We also need to recognize the new reality of the church — its cultural displacement and its institutional disarray. The viability of the church rests in God who created and sustains it. But the church, like the people who comprise it, does experience times of trial, weakness, and frailty. God does not protect disciples or the church from such moments in history. Such a time is now. What troubles us, however, is that some of mainstream Protestantism's current fragility is the result of self-inflicted wounds caused by our own adherents and by our limited agendas.

What the church needs now is to renew its commitment to nurture — to strengthen the faith and to sustain the Christian community, including its institutions. "Nurture" is a word with rich connotations. Nurturing parents help and challenge children to grow and mature. They recognize the necessity of helping their children see new visions of justice, truth, and love, but they also seek to instill in their offspring the importance of passing on enduring values. They exercise discipline but recognize the importance of freedom and autonomy. Nurturing parents seek to help their children become mature, responsible, and healthy adults.

We need to recover an understanding of nurture as central to the church's mission, rather than as a preparation for it. As Paul told the Ephesians, "The gifts [Christ] gave were that some would be apostles, some prophets, some evangelists, some pastors and teachers, to equip the saints for the work of ministry, for building up the body of Christ, until all of us come to the unity of the faith and of the knowledge of the Son of God, to maturity, to the measure of the full stature of Christ" (Eph. 4:11-13).

Here are four areas of nurture that the church needs to emphasize for its mission today:

➤ *Vital Sign: Nurturing Congregations*

Mainstream Protestant denominations are gradually adjusting to the organizational revolution that began in the 1950s. The process is painful, for it involves reconceiving not only the priorities but also the structures of denominations themselves. The need for such reorientation is imperative. The trust between congregations and denominational organizations which made the corporate denomination work so well has ebbed. Congregations no longer exist for denominational mission; denominations exist to nurture and strengthen the mission of congregations.

This strategy has obvious dangers. Focusing on congregations strengthens large churches at the expense of small congregations. Emphasizing congregations encourages the parochialism and localism which are such powerful forces in American society. We believe, however, that there are strong impulses within both congregations and the gospel itself that will counteract the tendency to look inward rather than outward. The task for denominations will be to inspire and encourage those congregational impulses to serve in mission throughout the world.[27]

➤ *Vital Sign: Nurturing Leaders*

In any organization in American society today, leadership is a complex responsibility, and it is particularly complex in the church.

As theological educators, we sometimes hear the complaint that today's pastors or priests are not as highly qualified as those of preceding generations. Quality is notoriously difficult to measure, but we will concede two points. Today's seminarians are less literate in the Bible and in theology and are also less informed or motivated by their denomination's theological convictions. They frequently are ill-prepared in the liberal arts and sciences and often seem unable to relate the Christian faith to other areas of knowledge. The lack of biblical and theological literacy is a product of mainstream Protestant church life; the lack of educational breadth is a result of changes in American higher education.

Religious leaders, especially pastors and priests, are expected to be adept at spiritual direction, knowledge of the Bible, preaching, classroom teaching, financial management, volunteer coordination, pastoral counseling, community organization, physical plant maintenance, home and hospital visitation, evangelistic outreach, and relating to all ages of adults and children. When they show they have clay feet, it should hardly be surprising in light of Christ's teaching about human fallibility.

The complications of modern life have heightened the demands on pastors and priests in all areas of the church's life. We have heard retired ministers express gratitude that they are not serving congregations today because congregations' expectations are so high and the resources for meeting them so limited. Lay leaders often experience the same pressures to do more, as well as the same anger and resentment when they cannot meet congregational needs.

These are, however, the leaders God has sent us for this hour. As in every age of the church's life, our leaders are inadequate to the task set before them. But we would do better to find ways of supporting and improving them, rather than finding ways to circumscribe their authority or undermine their effectiveness.

We should also look ahead and nurture the next generation of leaders for our churches. One of the casualties of the waning

Protestant ecosystems is the network of institutions and practices that identified and enlisted lay and ministerial leadership. The colleges, campus ministries, student or youth organizations, and conferences that once encouraged people to consider what was called "full-time Christian service" no longer exercise that same influence. Mainstream Protestant denominations have been conspicuously silent in calling forth their leaders; most seminarians are called by God but remain largely "self-selected" for ministry. Perhaps no other institution in American culture deals with the future of its leadership with such benign neglect as mainstream Protestant denominations.

We should identify the individuals in our congregations who have the gifts and talents for ministry, and we should invite them to consider this vocation. The invitation can be extended to youth and adults, but we suggest that special attention be given to junior and senior high school students as they begin to think about their life's work.

➤ *Vital Sign: Nurturing a New Ecosystem of Faith*

Some elements of the old ecosystem are dead. Clearly the public schools are not going to restore the earlier Protestant and Christian ethos. Legalized Sabbath observance is a political, legal, and cultural impossibility. Many Protestant social service organizations, such as hospitals, are long gone as bearers of Christian beliefs and values.

Nevertheless, the purpose of these parts of the ecosystem and the motivation for creating them are important. We should not rely upon the public schools to teach Christianity, but it remains critical that children grow in "the nurture and admonition of the Lord." We cannot rely upon the state to "remember the Sabbath and keep it holy," but it still is important for us to establish a discipline and rhythm to our life in Christ. We can no longer depend upon social service agencies to communicate the Christian faith, but that does not absolve us from meeting the spiritual and physical needs of people in our world. The question is not whether we do these things, but how.

Other parts of the ecosystem are still alive and can be renewed and reformed. Many of our expectations for the Sunday schools are beyond the reach of the most gifted teachers and the best curricula. But the Sunday school can still be effective for helping children and adults experience the excitement of discovering the breadth and depth of the Christian faith. Some church-related colleges are struggling to define their Christian identity in the secular academic world. Theological seminaries are crucial in training future leaders, both clergy and laity, and in transmitting the distinctive features of denominational traditions.

New vital signs of the ecosystems are also emerging, such as the small group movement, the special interest groups, and the social service programs mentioned earlier. Most of these vital signs have appeared in congregations and will likely continue to appear there in the future. Tomorrow's new ecosystems are being built within congregations, but congregations can play a critical role in expanding and strengthening these elements. In doing so, they will renew and redefine the nature of denominations.

➤ *Vital Sign: Nurturing Families and Their Faith*

We believe the most important vital sign in the new ecosystems of mainstream Protestantism will be the congregations' ministry with families. This does not mean, however, that the churches should abandon single people or idealize a nuclear family that no longer exists.

Instead, we recommend that the churches recognize families in all their complexity; virtually everyone has a family, according to some definition. We especially urge congregations to focus on children — whose status has been so endangered — by bringing them back in touch with parents and extended families under the umbrella of a commonly shared piety.

The columnist Ellen Goodman has written, "Without wallowing in false nostalgia, there has been a fundamental shift. Americans once expected parents to raise their children in accordance with the dominant cultural messages. Today they are expected to raise their children in opposition." Goodman reflects the anxieties and fears of parents who see the violent and inhumane values that cheapen life and human relationships. "It's what makes child-raising harder. It's why parents feel more isolated. It's not just that American families have less time with their kids, it's that we have to spend more of this time doing battle with our own culture."[28]

In turning away from the "old agenda" of issues related to families and individual behavior in the 1960s, we tragically lost an opportunity to address families with vibrant spiritual resources during a period in which they were experiencing tumultuous change. But if we can recover our concern for strengthening families, and help them be embodiments and bearers of Christian faith and community, we will address a central challenge of Christian nurture in our day.

In summary, in the midst of contention within our denominations and violent hatred in our world, we have a distinct calling. How we deal with conflict within the church can be a compelling Christian testimony in a world scarred by bloodshed, fear, and intolerance. In the midst of conflict in the church at Colossae, the apostle Paul wrote: "As God's chosen ones, holy and beloved, clothe yourselves with compassion, kindness, humility, meekness, and patience. Bear with one another and, if anyone has a complaint against another, forgive each other; just as the Lord has forgiven you, so you also must forgive. Above all, clothe yourselves with love, which binds everything together in perfect harmony" (Col. 3:12-14).

The church is ultimately God's gift to us. Love the church.

Love the Lord.

Most of the research on membership decline in mainstream Protestantism has emphasized the importance of sociological factors such as demographics. Some studies, however, conclude that the main problem for mainstream Protestant churches is theological. We agree, and the theological challenge confronting us is profound.[29]

Our history in the twentieth century is largely the story of the deep divisions spawned by conservative and liberal perspectives. The fundamentalist controversies posed the question of how sharply the boundaries of truth and orthodoxy would be defined. Conservatives insisted that the boundaries be clear, well defined, and defended. Liberals maintained that the church should be inclusive and embrace a variety of points of view.

The internecine civil war in twentieth-century American Protestantism was inevitable. As it continued, it became a convenient way of describing the Christian world. Each group became increasingly adept at defining its boundaries by saying what they were not. Liberals generally seized control of denominational agencies and theological seminaries, and virtually every mainstream Protestant denomination has witnessed a schism or the withdrawal of a conservative group.

Like the Cold War in international politics, each side viewed the other as a monolith. Points of common heritage and even agreement, as well as the complexity within each party, were overlooked. In trying to distance themselves from fundamentalism, mainstream Protestant leaders have often minimized the strength of evangelicalism in their past, and have suppressed the influence of evangelicals in their own denominations. As a result, mainstream Protestantism tends to be more hospitable to the novelty of the left, while undervaluing the traditionalists of the right.

> ### Vital Sign: The Challenge of Idolatry

The research on mainstream Protestantism reveals how tragic this civil war has been. As mainstream Protestants relied on the culture to reinforce Christian belief and values, the culture shaped us in its own image. We continued to see our primary threat coming from conservative Protestantism, failing to recognize the fragmenting of belief and values in modern society. One of the most important findings about the baby boom generation is that those who left mainstream Protestant churches embraced no subsequent church affiliation. As Roof and McKinney aptly conclude, the competition for mainstream Protestants "is not the conservatives [they have] *spurned* but the secularists [they have] *spawned*."[30]

In other words, we have been fighting the wrong enemy. Throughout the twentieth century, we have been preoccupied with combatting various forms of Christian belief (heresy) instead of combatting visions of life that are not religious at all (idolatry). Lesslie Newbigin calls secularism the "paganism of the West."[31] Throughout many parts of the world in the twentieth century totalitarianism has been the prevailing idolatry. The faith in technology that governs so much of our values is another form of the true threat to the Christian church in our age — the attempt to define life apart from God.

We believe there are several implications of defining the theological challenge of the church as the idolatry of secularism. The first and most obvious implication is that conservatives and liberals must recognize one another as Christians, rather than pariahs. If it has taught us anything, the twentieth century should have taught us that the church is ill-served by defining one another as non-Christian. There may not be much common ground between extreme fundamentalists and liberal Protestants, but there are rich resources in evangelical and mainstream Protestantism that can be shared.

We mainstream Protestants value toleration; we prize listening. It is time to listen to our sisters and brothers in Christ. In fact, we believe that the most important ecumenical issue of the late twentieth century is a renewed understanding and reconciliation between the conservative and liberal wings in Christianity. New occasions teach new duties.

Second, secularism is part of our churches, not a distant force to be engaged in the world. Critics within evangelical Protestantism sharply attack the movement for its capitulation to secularism, but we mainstream Protestants are particularly susceptible to secularism for several reasons. Enormous benefits have been achieved through science, social science, and technology. Mainstream Protestants have encouraged secular values in our schools and universities, both public and private, and in politics and society. Theologically, we affirm the goodness of God's creation and are therefore open to the ways in which secular knowledge may improve human welfare. We broke with what we saw as legalism and moralism in the name of toleration and freedom.

It is difficult to see the dangers of secularism because most of us believe in many of its benefits. The danger of secularism is its capacity to erode the vitality of Christian faith by relativizing and neutralizing Christ's claims on our individual and collective lives.

Some examples of the secularism within the church from our own experience may help illustrate its influence: Churches that sponsor youth groups for recreation because "the kids don't want to talk about religion"; congregations that object to a confession of sin in worship services because it makes people feel bad about themselves; a church retreat on renewing urban congregations that does not include any worship service; Bible study groups, modeled after the base communities in Central America, where the leader will not open with prayer because "that's the way fundamentalists do it."

Third, our response to secularism should include a renewal of worship. Secularization in American culture has not meant the decline of religion. Polls reveal that there has been virtually no change in religious belief in the last half-century.[32] It is religious behavior and affiliation that have changed, and mainstream Protestant churches have been especially affected by these shifts.

But the religious search continues; that is why Roof describes the churched and the unchurched baby boomers as "a generation of seekers."[33] The vitality of any church will consist in its ability to offer people ways to commune with God.

The critiques of contemporary worship are legion, and so are the prescriptions for renewal — better preaching, more contemporary music, experimental services, etc. Some of the innovations are helpful and necessary for engaging the sensibilities of people molded by the power of television and other mass media.

But the key to the renewal of worship, according to Leander Keck, "is restoring the integrity of worship — the praise of God." "Authentic praise of God acknowledges what is true about God; it responds to qualities that are 'there' and not simply 'there for me,'" Keck argues. In a world of suffering, "Praising God is the ultimate 'Nevertheless!' It is the supreme act of faith."[34]

It is also the supreme act of defiance against the secularism of the world. Amidst the contemporary individualism, relativism, and pluralism of modern societies, praising God compels us to recognize that we are not the measure of all things and that God's love and everlasting kindness are the final word about our human condition.

H. Richard Niebuhr put it this way: "We are in the grip of a power that neither asks our consent before it brings us into existence nor asks our agreement to continue us in being beyond our physical death."[35] Or in the simple words of the Puritan rhyme: "The God who made us saves us."

The church does one thing that no other institution can offer: it worships God. As the psalmist declared, "Worship the Lord in the beauty of holiness" (Ps. 29:2b, KJV).

Finally, we believe that secularism poses important challenges to our theology. In their study of baby boomers, Hoge, Johnson, and Luidens describe a powerful stream in mainstream Protestantism which they call "lay liberalism." It is a lay movement, they say, because it does not conform to any prevailing theological school. It is liberal because it accepts differences, tolerates uncertainties, endorses individualism, and espouses liberal positions on most social and political issues. "In a sense," they write, "it is more a methodology — one which assumes the validity of diversity — than an ideology. Lay liberals have come to terms with the multiple, often conflicting, cultural messages they receive in this world; they accept that variety in truth claims is essential."[36]

Lay liberals are conventional in their Christian beliefs, but they refuse to accept the exclusive truth of Christianity. For them, the Christian faith is true, but other ways of understanding God may also be true.

We suspect that lay liberalism is pervasive in more than simply the baby boom generation, for it symbolizes one part of the heritage of mainstream Protestantism in the twentieth century — for good or for ill. We are undoubtedly better off with a vision of Christianity in which the boundaries of faith are defined by God's love, rather than a conviction that God has consigned some to hell. Yet lay liberalism as a methodology erodes both the basis of the gospel and the confidence to proclaim it.

Hoge, Johnson, and Luidens discovered that the most powerful factor predicting church affiliation was belief. Their findings are a poignant and penetrating reminder of one of the central characteristics of the church: beliefs matter. Theology is important. Faith in the good news of Jesus Christ is at the heart of what it means to be Christian.[37]

➤ *Vital Sign: Confessing Jesus Christ as Lord*

Mainstream Protestantism, we believe, failed the baby boomers and many others by our facile acceptance of pluralism, our reluctance to make truth claims, and our uneasiness with the religious questions that propel the human search for God. In this sense, conservative churches succeeded because they kept asking the right questions, even if their answers were inadequate. The questions we need to continue asking include: Who is God? What is the authority for truth? Is there an answer to suffering and evil? Is there a meaning for life? Is there hope for this life? Is there another life after this one? Can I be forgiven? Can I be loved? These questions, and others like them, are the agonizing religious questions that drive people to seek answers through a community such as the church. When they are not addressed, or when they are discussed with ambivalence and studied ambiguity, people move on.

Hoge, Johnson, and Luidens declare, "If the mainline churches want to regain their vitality, their first step must be to address theological issues head-on. They must listen to the voices of the lay liberals and provide compelling answers to the question, 'What's so special about Christianity?' "[38]

What indeed is so special about Christianity? That question can only be answered in terms of the uniqueness of Jesus Christ. Christ's question, "Who do you say that I am?" (Matt. 16:15), has a particular urgency for mainstream Protestantism and is the crucial question for the renewal of theology in our tradition. For centuries, the church has debated how we should understand Jesus as the Christ. Indeed, movements for reform in the history of the church have always involved renewed inquiry into the mystery of the incarnation of God in Jesus Christ.

The church's past interpretations of who is Jesus Christ can undoubtedly enrich our exploration of Scripture. But the fact remains that the central issue for the church today is whether we confess that Jesus Christ is Lord. For mainstream Protestants, confessing Jesus as Lord means that we distinctively affirm that God loves this world — through creation, and through the life, death, and resurrection of Jesus. God so loved this world (Greek:

kosmos) that Jesus Christ was sent by God "so that everyone who believes in him may not perish but have eternal life" (John 3:16). In that famous encapsulation of the gospel lies the assurance that the world is not condemned, but is loved by God. This world will not be forever scarred by evil and injustice; it will, rather, be reconciled through Jesus Christ. In a world marked by so many divisions, this radical vision of Christ making creation one in communion with itself and with God is what the gospel means by salvation.

The idolatry of our age is secularism — defining life without reference to God. The Christian rejection of secularism involves confessing Jesus Christ as Lord, for only through God's love in Jesus Christ does the secular take on meaning and value.

Finally, sisters and brothers, as we look back on our past and forward into our future, we encourage you not to lose heart. In the midst of these turbulent times, we are being called to bear witness to God's power and love. As in ages past, such a witness will involve hardship and suffering, but we rely upon God's promise that we are not alone in this pilgrimage of faith.

The second letter to Timothy addressed a man who had inherited his faith both from his grandmother Lois and his mother Eunice. The admonition to Timothy is a summons to faith and witness which we need to hear and heed:

> Do not be ashamed, then, of the testimony about our Lord or of me his prisoner, but join with me in suffering for the gospel, relying on the power of God, who saved us and called us with a holy calling, not according to our works but according to his own purpose and grace. This grace was given to us in Christ Jesus before the ages began, but it has now been revealed through the appearing of our Savior Christ Jesus, who abolished death and brought life and immortality to light through the gospel. For this gospel I was appointed a herald and an apostle and a teacher, and for this reason I suffer as I do. But I am not ashamed, for I know the one in whom I have put my trust, and I am sure that he is able to guard until that day what I have entrusted to him. Hold to the standard of sound teaching that you have heard

from me, in the faith and love that are in Christ Jesus. Guard
the good treasure entrusted to you, with the help of the Holy
Spirit living in us. (2 Tim. 1:8-14)

That indeed is what is "so special about Christianity." Grace
be with you all.

In Christ,

Joe, John, and Louis

Notes

Introduction

1. Milton J Coalter, John M. Mulder, and Louis Weeks, eds., *The Presbyterian Predicament: Six Perspectives* (1990); *The Confessional Mosaic: Presbyterians and Twentieth-Century Theology* (1990); *The Mainstream Protestant "Decline": The Presbyterian Pattern* (1990); *The Diversity of Discipleship: Presbyterians and Twentieth-Century Christian Witness* (1991); *The Pluralistic Vision: Presbyterians and Mainstream Protestant Education and Leadership* (1992); *The Organizational Revolution: Presbyterians and American Denominationalism* (1992). These six volumes are summarized in *The Re-Forming Tradition: Presbyterians and Mainstream Protestantism* (1992). All seven volumes were published by Westminster/John Knox Press.

2. Kenneth L. Woodward, "Dead End for the Mainline?" *Newsweek*, 9 August 1993, pp. 46-48.

3. For discussions of the problem of defining "mainstream" or "mainline," see William R. Hutchison, ed., *Between the Times: The Travail of the Protestant Establishment in America, 1900–1960* (Cambridge: Cambridge University Press, 1989), pp. vii-xv, 3-18; W. Clark Roof and William McKinney, *American Mainline Religion: Its Changing Shape and Future* (New Brunswick, N.J.: Rutgers University Press, 1987), pp. 72-105.

4. Leonard Sweet, "Can a Mainstream Change Its Course?" in *Liberal Protestantism: Realities and Possibilities,* ed. Robert S. Michaelson and Wade Clark Roof (New York: Pilgrim Press, 1986), pp. 235-62.

5. Catherine Albanese, *America, Religions and Religion,* 2nd ed. (Belmont,

133

Calif.: Wadsworth, 1992); R. Laurence Moore, *Religious Outsiders and the Making of Americans* (New York: Oxford University Press, 1986).

6. Hutchison, *Between the Times*, pp. 141-230. For the statistics on Protestant church membership, see Kenneth B. Bedell, ed., *Yearbook of American and Canadian Churches, 1994* (Nashville: Abingdon, 1994), pp. 253-59.

7. These themes are developed at greater length in Coalter, Mulder, and Weeks, *The Re-Forming Tradition*, pp. 35-65.

8. Roger Finke and Rodney Stark, *The Churching of America, 1776–1990: Winners and Losers in Our Religious Economy* (New Brunswick, N.J.: Rutgers University Press, 1992); "How the Up-Start Sects Won America: 1776-1850," *Journal for the Scientific Study of Religion* 28 (1989): 27-44; R. Laurence Moore, *Selling God: American Religion in the Marketplace of Culture* (New York: Oxford University Press, 1994).

9. Martin E. Marty, *Modern American Religion: The Irony of It All, 1893–1919* (Chicago: University of Chicago Press, 1986), *American Religion: The Noise of Conflict, 1919-1941* (Chicago: University of Chicago Press, 1991), *Denominations at Century's End* (Grand Rapids, Mich.: Calvin College and Seminary, 1991).

10. Quoted by Jonathan J. Bonk, "Globalization and Mission Education," *Theological Education* 30 (1993): 47.

Chapter 1

1. John R. Mott, *The Evangelization of the World in This Generation* (New York: Student Volunteer Movement for Foreign Missions, 1900), p. 14.

2. Stephen L. Carter, *The Culture of Disbelief* (New York: Basic Books, 1993).

3. Anson Phelps Stokes, *Church and State in the United States*, vol. 3 (New York: Harper and Bros., 1950), p. 453.

4. Phillip E. Hammond, *Religion and Personal Autonomy: The Third Disestablishment in America* (Columbia, S.C.: University of South Carolina Press, 1992), *The Protestant Presence in Twentieth-Century America: Religion and Political Culture* (Albany: State University of New York Press, 1992); W. Clark Roof and William McKinney, *American Mainline Religion: Its Changing Shape and Future* (New Brunswick, N.J.: Rutgers University Press, 1987); Robert Wuthnow, *The Restructuring of American Religion: Society and Faith Since World War II* (Princeton: Princeton University Press, 1988), *The Struggle for America's Soul: Evangelicals, Liberals, and Secularism* (Grand Rapids, Mich.: Wm. B. Eerdmans Publishing Co., 1989). For a popular version of this theme, see Loren B. Mead, *The Once and Future Church: Reinventing the Congregation for a New Mission Frontier* (Washington, D.C.: Alban Institute, 1991).

5. Seymour Martin Lipset, *The First New Nation: The United States in Historical and Comparative Perspective* (New York: Doubleday & Co., Anchor

Books, 1967), pp. 159-192; John K. Wilson, "Religion under the State Constitutions, 1776–1800," *Journal of Church and State* 32 (1990): 753-773; Winthrop S. Hudson, *Religion in America,* 4th ed. (New York: Macmillan Publishing
Co., 1987), pp. 96-103; Edwin S. Gaustad, *Neither King Nor Prelate: Religion
and the New Nation, 1776–1826* (Grand Rapids, Mich.: Wm. B. Eerdmans Publishing Co., 1993).

6. The best summaries of this impulse are Robert T. Handy, *A Christian
America: Protestant Hopes and Historical Realities,* 2nd ed. (New York: Oxford
University Press, 1984); Martin E. Marty, *Protestantism in the United States:
Righteous Empire,* 2nd ed. (New York: Charles Scribner's Sons, 1986).

7. The term was first coined by Robert T. Handy, "The American Religious
Depression, 1925–1935," *Church History* 29 (1960): 3-16; reprinted in John M.
Mulder and John F. Wilson, eds., *Religion in American History* (Englewood
Cliffs, N.J.: Prentice-Hall, 1978), pp. 431-44. See also Handy, *A Christian
America,* pp. 159-84.

8. Hammond, *Religion and Personal Autonomy;* Wuthnow, *The Restructuring of American Religion,* and *The Struggle for America's Soul;* Roof and McKinney,
American Mainline Religion; William R. Hutchison, ed., *Between the Times: The
Travail of the Protestant Establishment in America, 1900–1960* (Cambridge: Cambridge University Press, 1989).

9. Robert H. Wiebe, *The Search for Order, 1877-1920* (New York: Hill &
Wang, 1967); Richard Hofstadter, *The Age of Reform: From Bryan to F.D.R.* (New
York: Vintage Books, 1955).

10. C. Howard Hopkins, *The Rise of the Social Gospel in American Protes-
tantism, 1865–1915* (New Haven: Yale University Press, 1940); Henry F. May,
Protestant Churches and Industrial America (New York: Harper & Bros., 1949);
Ronald C. White and C. Howard Hopkins, eds., *The Social Gospel: Religion and
Reform in Changing America* (Philadelphia: Temple University Press, 1976);
Susan Curtis, *A Consuming Faith: The Social Gospel and Modern American Culture*
(Baltimore: Johns Hopkins University Press, 1991); Jean Miller Schmidt, *Souls
or the Social Order: The Two-Party System in American Protestantism* (Brooklyn:
Carlson, 1991); Marty, *Righteous Empire;* David O. Moberg, *The Great Reversal:
Evangelism versus Social Concern* (New York: Lippincott, 1972).

11. Francis J. Sorauf, *The Wall of Separation: The Constitutional Politics of
Church and State* (Princeton: Princeton University Press, 1976); Wuthnow, *The
Restructuring of American Religion,* pp. 6-8, 317-19; Carter, *The Culture of
Disbelief;* Richard J. Neuhaus, *The Naked Public Square: Religion and Democracy in
America,* 2nd ed. (Grand Rapids, Mich.: Wm. B. Eerdmans Publishing Co., 1984).

12. Dennis N. Voskuil, "Reaching Out: Mainline Protestantism and the
Media," in *Between the Times,* pp. 72-92; J. W. Gregg Meister, "Presbyterians
and Mass Media: A Case of Blurred Vision and Missed Mission," in *The Diversity
of Discipleship: Presbyterians and Twentieth-Century Christian Witness,* ed. Milton J
Coalter, John M. Mulder, and Louis B. Weeks (Louisville, Ky.: Westminster/John
Knox Press, 1991), pp. 170-86.

13. Ibid.; Jeffrey K. Hadden and Charles E. Swann, *Prime-Time Preachers: The Rising Power of Televangelism* (Reading, Mass.: Addison-Wesley, 1981); Michael Lienesch, *Redeeming America: Piety and Politics in the New Christian Right* (Chapel Hill, N.C.: University of North Carolina Press, 1993); R. Laurence Moore, *Selling God: American Religion in the Marketplace of Culture* (New York: Oxford University Press, 1994); Razelle Frankl, *Televangelism: The Marketing of Popular Religion* (Carbondale, Ill.: University of Southern Illinois Press, 1987); William F. Fore, *Television and Religion: The Shaping of Faith, Values, and Culture* (Minneapolis: Augsburg, 1981); Jeffrey K. Hadden and Anson Shupe, *Televangelism: Power and Politics on God's Frontier* (New York: Henry Holt, 1988); Leonard I. Sweet, *Communication and Change in American Religious History* (Grand Rapids, Mich.: Wm. B. Eerdmans Publishing Co., 1993).

14. David B. Barrett, "Annual Statistical Table on Global Mission: 1994," *International Bulletin of Missionary Research* 18, no. 1 (1994): 24-25. Barrett's massive compilation of data is *World Christian Encyclopedia* (New York: Oxford University Press, 1981).

15. Barrett, "Annual Statistical Table on Global Mission: 1994," 24-25.

16. Vinson Synan, *The Holiness-Pentecostal Movement in the United States* (Grand Rapids, Mich.: Wm. B. Eerdmans Publishing Co., 1971); Donald W. Dayton, *Theological Roots of Pentecostalism* (Metuchen, N.J.: Scarecrow Press, 1987); Edith W. Blumhofer, *The Assemblies of God: A Chapter in the Story of American Pentecostalism* (Springfield, Mo.: Gospel Publishing House, 1980), *Restoring the Faith: The Assemblies of God, Pentecostalism, and American Culture* (Urbana, Ill.: University of Illinois Press, 1993); David Martin, *Tongues of Fire: The Explosion of Protestantism in Latin America* (Cambridge, Mass.: Basil Blackwell, 1990); Walter Hollenweger, *The Pentecostals* (London: SCM Press, 1972); Harvey Cox, *Fire From Heaven: The Rise of Pentecostal Spirituality and the Shaping of Religion in the Twenty-First Century* (New York: Addison-Wesley Publishing Co., 1995).

17. See, for example: Paul F. Knitter, ed., *Pluralism and Oppression: Theology in World Perspective* (Lanham, Md.: University Press of America, 1991); Kofi Appiah-Kubi and Sergio Torres, eds., *African Theology en Route* (Maryknoll, N.Y.: Orbis Books, 1983); Virginia Fabelaa, Peter K. H. Lee, David Kawng-sun Suh, *Asian Christian Spirituality: Reclaiming Traditions* (Maryknoll, N.Y.: Orbis, 1992); Gary H. Gossen, ed., *South and Meso-American Spirituality: From the Cult of the Feathered Serpent to the Theology of Liberation* (New York: Crossroad, 1993).

18. John Hick, *An Interpretation of Religion: Human Responses to the Transcendent* (New Haven: Yale University Press, 1989); John Hick and Paul F. Knitter, eds., *The Myth of Christian Uniqueness: Toward a Pluralistic Theology of Religions* (Maryknoll, N.Y.: Orbis Books, 1987); Diana Eck, *Encountering God: A Spiritual Journey From Bozeman to Banaras* (Boston: Beacon Press, 1993).

19. William Temple, *The Church Looks Forward* (New York: Macmillan Co., 1944), p. 2.

20. Samuel McCrea Cavert, *The American Churches in the Ecumenical*

Movement, 1900–1968 (New York: Association Press, 1968); Charles S. Mcfarland, *Christian Unity in the Making: The First Twenty-Five Years of the Federal Council of the Churches of Christ in America, 1905–1930* (New York: Federal Council of Churches of Christ in America, 1948); Ruth Rouse and Stephen C. Neill, *A History of the Ecumenical Movement,* vol. 1, 2nd ed. (Philadelphia: Westminster Press, 1967), *A History of the Ecumenical Movement,* vol. 2, ed. Harold E. Fey (Philadelphia: Westminster Press, 1970); Mark A. Noll, *A History of Christianity in the United States and Canada* (Grand Rapids, Mich.: Wm. B. Eerdmans Publishing Co., 1992), pp. 535-40.

For two analyses of Presbyterian ecumenism, see Theodore A. Gill, Jr., "American Presbyterians in the Global Ecumenical Movement;" and Erskine Clarke, "Presbyterian Ecumenical Activity in the United States," in *The Diversity of Discipleship,* pp. 126-48, 149-69.

21. Jay P. Dolan, *The American Catholic Experience: A History from Colonial Times to the Present* (Garden City, N.Y.: Doubleday & Co., 1985), pp. 424-25, 433-34.

22. George Gallup, Jr. and Jim Castelli, *The People's Religion: American Faith in the 1990s* (New York: Macmillan, 1989), pp. 186-88.

23. *Faith Development and Your Ministry,* a report on a Gallup survey conducted for the Religious Education Association of the U.S. and Canada by the Princeton Religion Research Center, Princeton, N.J., table 13, pp. 16-17.

24. The literature on fundamentalism is extensive; among the most important works are George M. Marsden, *Fundamentalism and American Culture: The Shaping of Twentieth-Century Evangelicalism, 1820–1925* (New York: Oxford University Press, 1980), *Reforming Fundamentalism: Fuller Seminary and the New Evangelicalism* (Grand Rapids, Mich.: Wm. B. Eerdmans Publishing Co., 1987), *Understanding Fundamentalism and Evangelicalism* (Grand Rapids, Mich.: Wm. B. Eerdmans Publishing Co., 1991); Ernest R. Sandeen, *The Roots of Fundamentalism: British and American Millenarianism, 1820–1925* (New York: Oxford University Press, 1980); Nancy Tatom Ammerman, *Bible Believers: Fundamentalists in the Modern World* (New Brunswick, N.J.: Rutgers University Press, 1987); Martin E. Marty and R. Scott Appleby, eds., *Fundamentalisms Observed* (Chicago: University of Chicago Press, 1991), *Fundamentalism and Society: Reclaiming the Sciences, the Family, and Education* (Chicago: University of·Chicago Press, 1993), and *Fundamentalisms and the State* (Chicago: University of Chicago Press, 1993), vols. 1, 2, and 3 of *The Fundamentalism Project.*

25. Cited in Marsden, *Fundamentalism and American Culture,* p. 188.

26. See works cited in n. 24.

27. Roof and McKinney, *American Mainline Religion,* pp. 186-228; Marsden, *Understanding Fundamentalism and Evangelicalism,* pp. 62-82; Wuthnow, "The Restructuring of American Presbyterianism: Turmoil in One Denomination," in *The Presbyterian Predicament: Six Perspectives,* ed. Milton J Coalter, John M. Mulder, and Louis B. Weeks (Louisville, Ky.: Westminster/John Knox Press, 1990), pp. 27-48.

28. James Davison Hunter, *Culture Wars: The Struggle to Define America* (New York: Basic Books, 1991), *Before the Shooting Begins* (New York: Free Press, 1994); Peter Berger, "The Class Struggle in American Religion," *Christian Century* 98 (25 February 1981): 194-99, "Different Gospels: The Social Sources of Apostasy," in *American Apostasy: The Triumph of "Other" Gospels,* ed. Richard John Neuhaus (Grand Rapids, Mich.: Wm. B. Eerdmans Publishing Co., 1989), pp. 1-14.

29. Wuthnow, *The Struggle for America's Soul.*

30. Coalter, Mulder, and Weeks, *The Re-Forming Tradition,* pp. 273-87; Robert Wuthnow, *Christianity in the Twenty-First Century: Reflections on the Challenges Ahead* (New York: Oxford University Press, 1993), pp. 134-35.

31. Monika E. Giddy of the Holland, Michigan public schools supplied the data on Holland; Leon F. Bouvier and Cary B. Davis, *Immigration and the Future Racial Composition of the United States* (Alexandria, Va.: Center for Immigration Research and Education, 1982), pp. 7-19.

32. Roof and McKinney, *American Mainline Religion,* p. 142.

33. Barbara Brown Zikmund, "Ministry of Word and Sacrament: Women and Changing Understandings of Ordination," in *The Presbyterian Predicament,* pp. 134-58; Barbara J. MacHaffie, *Her Story: Women in Christian Tradition* (Philadelphia: Fortress Press, 1986); Elizabeth H. Verdesi, *In but Still Out: Women in the Church* (Philadelphia: Westminster Press, 1976); Patricia R. Hill, *The World Their Household: The American Woman's Foreign Mission Movement and Cultural Transformation, 1870–1920* (Ann Arbor: University of Michigan Press, 1985); John P. McDowell, *The Social Gospel in the South: The Woman's Home Mission Movement in the Methodist Episcopal Church, South, 1886–1936* (Baton Rouge, La.: Louisiana State University Press, 1982); Nancy F. Cott, ed., *History of Women in the United States: Religion* (Munich: K. G. Saur, 1993).

34. See, for example, the essays on Presbyterian African-Americans, Native Americans, Hispanic Americans, Japanese-Americans, and Korean-Americans in *The Diversity of Discipleship,* pp. 187-330.

35. *Gallup Opinion Index: Special Report on Religion* (February 1969); Roof found that 28% of the baby boomers also hold this belief. *A Generation of Seekers,* pp. 71, 202.

36. Dean R. Hoge, Benton Johnson, and Donald A. Luidens, *Vanishing Boundaries: The Religion of Mainline Protestant Baby Boomers* (Louisville, Ky.: Westminster/John Knox Press, 1994), pp. 140-41; Roof and McKinney, *American Mainline Religion,* p. 43; Robert N. Bellah, et al., *Habits of the Heart* (Berkeley: University of California Press, 1985), p. 221.

37. Edwin Scott Gaustad, *Historical Atlas of Religion in America,* rev. ed. (New York: Harper & Row, 1976), pp. 87, 165, 166; Roger Finke and Rodney Stark, "Turning Pews into People: Estimating Nineteenth-Century Church Membership," *Journal for the Scientific Study of Religion* 25 (1986): 180-92. See also Jon Butler, *Awash in a Sea of Faith* (Cambridge: Harvard University Press, 1990), pp. 257-58.

38. Roof and McKinney, *American Mainline Religion,* pp. 69, 162-81, 184-85; Wuthnow, *The Restructuring of American Religion,* pp. 88-91, 170-71;

Hoge, Johnson, and Luidens, *Vanishing Boundaries,* pp. 49, 123, 168, 171; Roof, *A Generation of Seekers,* pp. 151-81.

39. Hoge, Johnson, and Luidens, *Vanishing Boundaries,* pp. 175-212.

40. Winthrop S. Hudson, "Denominationalism as a Basis for Ecumenicity: A Seventeenth-Century Conception," *Church History* 24 (1955): 32-50, reprinted in Russell E. Richey, ed., *Denominationalism* (Nashville: Abingdon Press, 1977), pp. 21-49.

41. Coalter, Mulder, and Weeks, *The Re-Forming Tradition,* pp. 91-116; Russell E. Richey and Robert Bruce Mullin, introduction to *Reimagining Denominationalism: Interpretive Essays,* ed. Richey and Mullin (New York: Oxford University Press, 1994), pp. 3-11; Richey, "Denominations and Denominationalism: An American Morphology," in ibid., pp. 74-98; Richey, "Institutional Forms of Religion," in *Encyclopedia of Religion in America,* 3 vols., ed. Charles H. Lippy and Peter W. Williams (New York: Charles Scribner's Sons, 1988), 1:31-50.

42. Sidney E. Mead, *The Lively Experiment* (New York: Harper & Row, 1963), pp. 103-33.

43. See, for example, David Lyon, *The Steeple's Shadow: On the Myths and Realities of Secularization* (Grand Rapids, Mich.: Wm. B. Eerdmans Publishing Co., 1985); Jeffrey K. Hadden and Anson Shupe, eds., *Secularization and Fundamentalism Reconsidered* (New York: Paragon House, 1989).

44. For an understanding of modernization, see Peter L. Berger, Brigitte Berger, and Hansfried Kellner, *The Homeless Mind: Modernization and Consciousness* (New York: Random House, 1973); S. N. Eisenstadt, ed., *The Protestant Ethic and Modernization: A Comparative View* (New York: Basic Books, 1968); Richard D. Brown, *Modernization: The Transformation of American Life, 1600–1865* (New York: Hill & Wang, 1976). A similar interpretation stresses the "privatization" of religion in American culture; see John F. Wilson, "The Sociological Study of American Religion," in *Encyclopedia of the American Religious Experience,* 1:27-28.

45. H. Richard Niebuhr, *Christ and Culture* (New York: Harper & Row, 1951).

46. Martin E. Marty, "From the Centripetal to the Centrifugal in Culture and Religion," *Theology Today* 51 (1994): 5-16.

47. For a different theological vision of mainstream Protestantism, see Stanley Hauerwas and William H. Willimon, *Resident Aliens: Life in the Christian Colony* (Nashville: Abingdon Press, 1989).

Chapter 2

1. Martin E. Marty, foreword to *Understanding Church Growth and Decline 1950-1978,* ed. Dean R. Hoge and David A. Roozen (New York: Pilgrim Press, 1979), p. 12.

2. David A. Roozen and C. Kirk Hadaway, eds., *Church and Denominational Growth: What Does (and Does Not) Cause Growth or Decline* (Nashville: Abingdon, 1993), Appendix, Table A1.2, pp. 96-97.

3. Roozen and Hadaway, *Church and Denominational Growth,* Appendix, Table A1.1, p. 395.

4. William R. Hutchison, "Past Imperfect: History and the Prospect for Liberalism," in *Liberal Protestantism: Realities and Possibilities,* ed. Robert S. Michaelson and Wade Clark Roof (New York: Pilgrim Press, 1986), pp. 65-82.

5. For a discussion of the pruning theory, see Warren J. Hartman, *Membership Trends: A Study of Decline and Growth in the United Methodist Church 1949–1975* (Nashville: Discipleship Resources, 1976), p. 2; and Presbyterian Committee, *Membership Trends* (New York: United Presbyterian Church in the U.S.A., 1976), p. 226. For a discussion of the poor leadership theory, see J. Edward Carothers, *The Paralysis of Mainstream Protestant Leadership* (Nashville: Abingdon Press, 1990); and Donald A. Luidens, "Between Myth and Hard Data: A Denomination Struggles with Identity," in *Beyond Establishment: Protestant Identity in a Post-Protestant Age,* ed. Jackson W. Carroll and Wade Clark Roof (Louisville, Ky.: Westminster/John Knox Press, 1993), pp. 248-69. The claim that mainstream Protestants should seek to be more relevant can be found in William F. Starr, "The Changing Campus Scene: From Church to Coffeehouse," in *Never Trust a God Over 30,* ed. Albert H. Friedlander (New York: McGraw-Hill Book Co., 1967), p. 60; and General Assembly, Presbyterian Church in the United States, *Minutes,* 1970, part 1, p. 26. Several others have proposed that the problem was too much activism in the political and social arena: Jeffrey K. Hadden, *The Gathering Storm in the Churches: The Widening Gap Between Clergy and Laity* (Garden City, N.Y.: Doubleday & Co., 1969); Dean R. Hoge, *Division in the Protestant House: The Basic Reasons Behind Intra-Church Conflicts* (Philadelphia: Westminster Press, 1976), ch. 5; and Peter L. Berger, "American Religion: Conservative Upsurge, Liberal Prospects," in *Liberal Protestantism,* pp. 19-36.

6. These conclusions are explained in the Presbyterian case study in Milton J Coalter, John M. Mulder, and Louis B. Weeks, eds., *The Re-Forming Tradition: Presbyterians and Mainstream Protestantism* (Louisville, Ky.: Westminster/John Knox Press, 1992), pp. 67-90.

7. Wade Clark Roof, *A Generation of Seekers: The Spiritual Journeys of the Baby Boom Generation* (San Francisco: Harper, 1993), p. 2.

8. Wade Clark Roof and William McKinney, *American Mainline Religion: Its Changing Shape and Future* (New Brunswick, N.J.: Rutgers University Press), pp. 160-61.

9. Dennison Nash, "A Little Child Shall Lead Them: A Statistical Test of the Hypothesis that Children Were the Source of the American 'Religious Revival,'" *Journal for the Scientific Study of Religion* 7 (1968): 238-40.

10. Dean R. Hoge, Benton Johnson, and Donald A. Luidens, *Vanishing Boundaries: The Religion of Mainline Protestant Baby Boomers* (Louisville, Ky.: Westminster/John Knox Press, 1994), pp. 46-47, 55-56, 168; for an excellent

review, see James W. Lewis, "Baby Boomers: The Lapsed and the Loyal," *Christian Century* 111 (18 May 1994): 534-37. See also Robert Bellah et al., *Habits of the Heart: Individualism and Commitment in American Life* (New York: Harper & Row, 1986).

11. Hoge, Johnson, and Luidens, *Vanishing Boundaries,* pp. 50-55; Roof and McKinney, *American Mainline Religion,* pp. 170-71, 182.

12. Hoge, Johnson, and Luidens, *Vanishing Boundaries,* pp. 71-72.

13. Ibid., p. 71.

14. Roof, *Generation of Seekers,* p. 155.

15. Ibid., pp. 156-57; Hoge, Johnson, and Luidens, *Vanishing Boundaries,* p. 204; Wade Clark Roof and Sr. Mary Johnson, "Baby Boomers and the Return to the Churches," in *Church and Denominational Growth,* pp. 293-310.

16. Jerry Adler, "Kids Growing Up Scared," *Newsweek,* 10 January 1994, p. 44.

17. Presbyterian Church (USA), *The Presbyterian Panel: 1991–1993 Background Report* (Louisville, Ky.: Presbyterian Church [USA] Research Services, n.d.), pp. 20-21; and Hoge, Johnson, and Luidens, *Vanishing Boundaries,* pp. 130, 135, 154.

18. *Statistical Abstract of the United States, 1952,* p. 941; ibid., 1992, p. 17.

19. Roof and McKinney, *American Mainline Religion,* pp. 69, 162-85; Robert Wuthnow, *The Restructuring of American Religion: Society and Faith Since World War II* (Princeton: Princeton University Press, 1988), pp. 88-91, 170-71; Hoge, Johnson, and Luidens, *Vanishing Boundaries,* pp. 49, 123, 168, 175-212; and Roof, *Generation of Seekers,* pp. 151-81.

20. Roof and McKinney, *American Mainline Religion,* pp. 177-79.

21. Ibid.

22. Ibid., pp. 40-71.

23. Ibid., pp. 56-57.

24. Roof, *Generation of Seekers,* pp. 241-62.

25. James Hudnut-Beumler, *Looking for God in the Suburbs: The Religion of the American Dream and Its Critics* (New Brunswick, N.J.: Rutgers University Press, 1994); Thomas C. Berg, "'Proclaiming Together'? Convergence and Divergence in Mainline and Evangelical Evangelism, 1945-1967," *Religion and American Culture* 5 (1995): 49-76.

26. Bruce A. Greer, "Strategies for Evangelism and Growth in Three Denominations (1965–1990)," in *Church and Denominational Growth,* pp. 87-111; and Milton J Coalter, "Presbyterian Evangelism: A Case of Parallel Allegiances Diverging," in *The Diversity of Discipleship: Presbyterians and Twentieth-Century Christian Witness,* ed. Milton J Coalter, John M. Mulder, and Louis B. Weeks (Louisville, Ky.: Westminster/John Knox Press, 1991), pp. 33-54.

27. Bruce A. Greer, "Strategies for Evangelism and Growth in Three Denominations (1965–1990)," in *Church and Denominational Growth,* pp. 87-111.

28. Ibid.; Penny Long Marler and C. Kirk Hadaway, "New Church Development and Denominational Growth (1950–1988)," in ibid., pp. 47-86.

29. Jerrold Lee Brooks, "Reaching Out: A Study of Church Extension Activity in Mecklenburg Presbytery, North Carolina, 1920–1980," in *The Mainstream Protestant "Decline": The Presbyterian Pattern,* ed. Milton J Coalter, John M. Mulder, and Louis B. Weeks (Louisville, Ky.: Westminster/John Knox Press, 1990), pp. 177-97; and Robert H. Bullock, "Twentieth-Century Presbyterian New Church Development: A Critical Period, 1940–1980," in *Diversity of Discipleship,* pp. 55-82.

30. Greer, "Strategies for Evangelism and Growth in Three Denominations," 103; Bullock, "Twentieth-Century Presbyterian New Church Development," pp. 71-82.

31. Donald A. McGavran, *Understanding Church Growth,* 3rd ed., rev. and ed. C. Peter Wagner (Grand Rapids, Mich.: Wm. B. Eerdmans Publishing Co., 1990); Charles Van Engen, *The Growth of the True Church: An Analysis of the Ecclesiology of Church Growth Theory* (Amsterdam: Rodopi, 1981); Lesslie Newbigin, *The Open Secret: Sketches for a Missionary Theology* (Grand Rapids, Mich.: Wm. B. Eerdmans Publishing Co., 1978); Darrell L. Guder, "Evangelism and the Debate Over Church Growth," *Interpretation* 48 (1994): 145-55.

32. United Presbyterian Church in the United States of America, General Assembly, *Minutes,* part 1, pp. 293, 294.

33. Hoge and Roozen, *Understanding Church Growth and Decline,* pp. 160-78.

34. Ibid., p. 324; Hoge, Johnson, and Luidens, *Vanishing Boundaries,* pp. 10-11; and Wayne L. Thompson, Jackson W. Carroll, and Dean R. Hoge, "Growth or Decline in Presbyterian Congregations," in *Church and Denominational Growth,* pp. 196-97.

35. Hoge, Johnson, and Luidens, *Vanishing Boundaries,* pp. 177-78; and Thompson, Carroll, and Hoge, "Growth or Decline in Presbyterian Congregations," in *Church and Denominational Growth,* p. 198.

36. William D. Hendricks, *Exit Interviews: Revealing Stories of Why People Are Leaving the Church* (Chicago: Moody Press, 1993).

37. Daniel V. A. Olson, "Congregational Growth and Decline in Indiana Among Five Mainline Denominations," in *Church and Denominational Growth,* pp. 222-23.

38. Loren B. Mead, *More than Numbers: The Ways Churches Grow* (Washington: Alban Institute, 1993).

39. Olson, "Congregational Growth and Decline," in *Church and Denominational Growth,* pp. 221-23.

40. Jackson W. Carroll, *As One With Authority: Reflective Leadership in Ministry* (Louisville, Ky.: Westminster/John Knox Press, 1991), pp. 94-95.

41. Roy M. Oswald and Speed B. Leas, *The Inviting Church: A Study of New Member Assimilation* (New York: The Alban Institute, 1987), p. 44.

42. George Barna, *Marketing the Church* (Colorado Springs, Colo.: NavPress, 1988); George Barna, *A Step-By-Step Guide to Church Marketing: Breaking Ground for the Harvest* (Ventura, Calif.: Regal Books, 1992); C. Peter

Wagner, ed., *Church Growth: State of the Art* (Wheaton, Ill.: Tyndale House Publishers, 1988); McGavran, *Understanding Church Growth;* and Donald A. McGavran, *Ten Steps to Church Growth* (San Francisco: Harper & Row, 1977).

43. Penny Long Marler and David A. Roozen, "From Church Tradition to Consumer Choice: The Gallup Surveys of the Unchurched American," in *Church and Denominational Growth,* pp. 253-77.

44. Roozen and Hadaway, *Church and Denominational Growth,* p. 299.

45. Hoge, Johnson, and Luidens, *Vanishing Boundaries,* pp. 181, 205; Johnson, Hoge, and Luidens, "Mainline Churches: The Real Reason for Decline," *First Things* 31 (1993): 15.

Chapter 3

1. Alexander Campbell, *The Christian System . . .* (Nashville: Gospel Advocate Company, 1956), pp. 2, 3, 6.

2. Daniel Yankelovich, *New Rules: Searching for Self-Fulfillment in a World Turned Upside Down* (New York: Random House, 1981), pp. 4-5, cited by Wade Clark Roof, *A Generation of Seekers: The Spiritual Journeys of the Baby Boom Generation* (San Francisco: Harper, 1993), p. 44.

3. Paul A. Carter, *The Spiritual Crisis of the Gilded Age* (DeKalb, Ill.: Northern Illinois University Press, 1971). The description was coined by Arthur M. Schlesinger, Sr., in "A Critical Period in American Religion, 1875–1900," in *Massachusetts Historical Society Proceedings 64 (1930–32),* reprinted in John M. Mulder and John F. Wilson, eds., *Religion in American History* (Englewood Cliffs, N.J.: Prentice-Hall, 1978), pp. 302-17; Sydney Ahlstrom, *A Religious History of the American People* (New Haven: Yale University Press, 1972), p. 736. Ahlstrom shifted the description from "*a* critical period" to "*the* critical period."

4. William G. McLoughlin, *The Meaning of Henry Ward Beecher: An Essay on the Shifting Values of Mid-Victorian America* (New York: Alfred A. Knopf, 1970); William R. Hutchison, ed., *Between the Times: The Travail of the Protestant Establishment in America, 1900–1960* (Cambridge: Cambridge University Press, 1989), p. 4.

5. James Bryce, *The American Commonwealth,* 2 vols. (New York, 1910), 2:770, quoted in Robert T. Handy, *A Christian America: Protestant Hopes and Historical Realities,* 2nd ed. (New York: Charles Scribner's Sons, 1986), p. 99.

6. *Statistical Abstract of the United States, U.S. Department of Commerce, 1992,* p. 10.

7. Carl N. Degler, *The Age of the Economic Revolution, 1876–1900* (Glenview, Ill.: Scott, Foresman, 1967), p. 31.

8. Carter, *The Spiritual Crisis of the Gilded Age;* Schlesinger, "A Critical Period in American Religion"; R. Laurence Moore, "Secularization: Religion and the Social Sciences"; and Grant Wacker, "A Plural World: The Protestant Awak-

ening to World Religions," in *Between the Times,* pp. 233-77; Richard Hughes Seager, *The World's Parliament of Religions: The East/West Encounter, Chicago, 1893* (Bloomington, Ind.: Indiana University Press, 1994).

9. Quoted in John M. Mulder, *Woodrow Wilson: The Years of Preparation* (Princeton: Princeton University Press, 1978), pp. 106-7.

10. George M. Marsden, *Fundamentalism and American Culture: The Shaping of Twentieth-Century Evangelicalism, 1820–1925* (New York: Oxford University Press, 1980), and *Understanding Fundamentalism and Evangelicalism* (Grand Rapids, Mich.: Wm. B. Eerdmans Publishing Co., 1991).

11. Ibid. See also Ernest R. Sandeen, *The Roots of Fundamentalism: British and American Millenarianism, 1820–1925* (New York: Oxford University Press, 1980).

12. William R. Hutchison, *The Modernist Impulse in American Protestantism* (Cambridge: Harvard University Press, 1976).

13. See chap. 1, n. 9.

14. Lefferts A. Loetscher, *The Broadening Church* (Philadelphia: University of Pennsylvania Press, 1957); Bradley J. Longfield, *The Presbyterian Controversy: Fundamentalists, Modernists, and Moderates* (New York: Oxford University Press, 1991); John M. Mulder and Lee A. Wyatt, "The Predicament of Pluralism: The Study of Theology in Presbyterian Seminaries since the 1920s," in *The Pluralistic Vision: Presbyterians and Mainstream Protestant Education and Leadership,* ed. Milton J Coalter, John M. Mulder, and Louis B. Weeks (Louisville, Ky.: Westminster/John Knox Press, 1992), pp. 37-70.

15. Milton J Coalter, John M. Mulder, and Louis B. Weeks, eds., *The Re-Forming Tradition: Presbyterians and Mainstream Protestantism* (Louisville, Ky.: Westminster/John Knox Press, 1992), pp. 117-44.

16. Ahlstrom, *A Religious History of the American People,* pp. 873-964.

17. Mulder and Wyatt, "The Predicament of Pluralism," in *The Pluralistic Vision,* pp. 41-51; Dennis Voskuil, "Neo-Orthodoxy," in *Encyclopedia of the American Religious Experience,* 3 vols., ed. Charles H. Lippy and Peter W. Williams (New York: Charles Scribner's Sons, 1988), pp. 1147-57.

18. James H. Moorhead, "Theological Interpretations and Critiques of American Society and Culture," and Deane William Ferm, "Religious Thought Since World War II," in *Encyclopedia of the American Religious Experience,* pp. 101-15, 1159-72; Jack B. Rogers and Donald K. McKim, "Pluralism and Policy in Presbyterian Views of Scripture," and James H. Moorhead, "Redefining Confessionalism: American Presbyterians in the Twentieth Century," in *The Confessional Mosaic,* ed. Milton J Coalter, John M. Mulder, and Louis B. Weeks (Louisville, Ky.: Westminster/John Knox Press, 1990), pp. 37-58, 59-83; David L. Johnson and Charles E. Hambrick-Stowe, eds., *Theology and Identity: Traditions, Movements, and Polity in the United Church of Christ* (New York: Pilgrim Press, 1990); Alan G. Padgett, "Methodist Theology Today: A Review Essay of Thomas C. Oden, Systematic Theology," *Evangelical Quarterly* 64 (July 1992): 245-50; Thomas A. Langford, ed., *What Should Methodists Teach? Wesleyan Tradition and Modern Diversity* (Nashville: Kingswood Books, 1990).

19. H. Richard Niebuhr, *The Kingdom of God in America* (New York: Harper & Row, 1937), p. 193.

20. John A. Mackay, "Our Aims," *Theology Today* 1 (1944): 3-4.

21. See nn. 17 and 18.

22. The dominance of the neo-orthodox perspective is made clear in the following: Hutchison, *Between the Times,* pp. 19-140; Theodore A. Gill, Jr., "American Presbyterians in the Global Ecumenical Movement," in *The Diversity of Discipleship,* ed. Milton J Coalter, John M. Mulder, and Louis B. Weeks (Louisville, Ky.: Westminster/John Knox Press, 1991), pp. 126-48; John McClure, "Changes in the Authority, Method, and Message of Presbyterian (PCUSA) Preaching in the Twentieth Century"; Beverly Ann Zink, "Themes in Southern Presbyterian Preaching, 1920 to 1983"; Ronald P. Byars, "Challenging the Ethos: A History of Presbyterian Worship Resources in the Twentieth Century"; Morgan F. Simmons, "Hymnody: Its Place in Twentieth-Century Presbyterianism"; Mark A. Noll and Darryl G. Hart, "The Language(s) of Zion: Presbyterian Devotional Literature in the Twentieth Century"; in *The Confessional Mosaic,* pp. 84-207.

For an analysis of theological changes among the Disciples of Christ, see D. Newell Williams, *A Case Study of Mainstream Protestantism: The Disciples' Relation to American Culture, 1880–1980* (Grand Rapids, Mich.: Wm. B. Eerdmans Publishing Co., 1991), pp. 3-164.

Neo-orthodoxy certainly grew deep roots in mainstream Protestantism's leadership, and for this reason its theological themes were displayed prominently in the published literature of these denominations. Biblical criticism was likewise accepted by leaders, but as James Smart's *The Strange Silence of the Bible in the Churches* illustrated, what the leadership adopts may not take root among the rank and file.

23. David Harrington Watt, *A Transforming Faith: Explorations in Twentieth-Century American Evangelicalism* (New Brunswick, N.J.: Rutgers University Press, 1991); Joel Carpenter, *Revive Us Again: The Recovery of American Fundamentalism* (New York: Oxford University Press, 1991); Susan D. Rose, *Keeping Them Out of the Hands of Satan: Evangelical Schooling in America* (New York: Routledge, 1988); Virginia Lieson Brereton, *Training God's Army: The American Bible School, 1880–1940* (Bloomington, Ind.: Indiana University Press, 1990). For a case study of a conservative Presbyterian schism, see Rick Nutt, "The Tie That No Longer Binds: The Origins of the Presbyterian Church in America," in *The Confessional Mosaic,* pp. 236-56.

24. Ibid. See also George M. Marsden, *Reforming Fundamentalism: Fuller Seminary and the New Evangelicalism* (Grand Rapids, Mich.: Wm. B. Eerdmans Publishing Co., 1987); Carol Flake, *Redemptorama: Culture, Politics, and the New Evangelicalism* (New York: Penguin Books, 1984); Nancy Tatom Ammerman, *Bible Believers: Fundamentalists in the Modern World* (New Brunswick, N.J.: Rutgers University Press, 1987); James Davison Hunter, *American Evangelicalism: Conservative Religion and the Quandary of Modernity* (New Brunswick, N.J.: Rutgers University Press, 1983), *Evangelicalism: The New Generation* (Chicago:

University of Chicago Press, 1987); Timothy P. Weber, "Fundamentalism Twice Removed: The Emergence and Shape of Progressive Evangelicalism," in *New Dimensions in American Religious History,* ed. Jay P. Dolan and James P. Wind (Grand Rapids, Mich.: Wm. B. Eerdmans Publishing Co., 1993), pp. 261-87.

25. Moorhead, "Theological Interpretations and Critiques of American Society and Culture"; Ferm, "Religious Thought Since World War II"; Glenn T. Miller and Robert Wood Lynn, "Christian Theological Education"; in *Encyclopedia of the American Religious Experience,* pp. 101-15, 1159-72, 1627-52; James H. Gustafson, "Christian Ethics," in *Religion,* ed. Paul Ramsey (Englewood Cliffs, N.J.: Prentice-Hall, 1965), pp. 285-354.

26. G. J. Slosser, *Christian Unity* (New York: E. P. Dutton & Co., 1929); Peter Ainslie, *The Scandal of Christianity* (Chicago: Willett, Clark, & Colby, 1929); H. Richard Niebuhr, *The Social Sources of Denominationalism* (New York: Henry Holt and Co., 1929).

27. A. Roy Eckardt, *The Surge of Piety in America: An Appraisal* (New York: Association Press, 1958), p. 154; Will Herberg, *Protestant, Catholic, Jew* (New York: Doubleday & Co., 1956); Peter L. Berger, *The Noise of Solemn Assemblies: Christian Commitment and Religious Establishment in America* (Garden City, N.Y.: Doubleday & Co., 1961); Gibson Winter, *The Suburban Captivity of the Churches* (Garden City, N.Y.: Doubleday & Co., 1961); Martin E. Marty, *The New Shape of American Religion* (New York: Harper & Row, 1959).

28. Ahlstrom, *A Religious History of the American People,* pp. 947-48; Moorhead, "Redefining Confessionalism," in *The Confessional Mosaic,* p. 66.

29. James Hudnut-Beumler, *Looking for God in the Suburbs: The Religion of the American Dream and Its Critics* (New Brunswick, N.J.: Rutgers University Press, 1994).

30. Ahlstrom, "The Radical Turn in Theology and Ethics: Why It Occurred in the 1960s," in *Religion in American History,* p. 446; Ahlstrom, *A Religious History of the American People,* pp. 1079-99.

31. Jay P. Dolan, *The American Catholic Experience: A History from Colonial Times to the Present* (Garden City, N.Y.: Doubleday & Co., 1985), pp. 424, 433-34.

32. Ahlstrom, *A Religious History of the American People,* pp. 1009-18, 1085; see also the fiftieth anniversary articles in *Theological Studies* 50 (1989) which survey the changes in twentieth-century Catholic biblical scholarship, and Gerald P. Fogarty, S.J., "American Catholic Biblical Scholarship," in *Altered Landscapes,* pp. 226-45.

33. James H. Cone, "Black Religious Thought," in *Encyclopedia of the American Religious Experience,* pp. 1173-87. The best introduction to black theology of the 1960s and 1970s is Gayraud S. Wilmore and James H. Cone, eds., *Black Theology: A Documentary History, 1966–1979* (Maryknoll, N.Y.: Orbis Books, 1979). See also the fine survey by C. Eric Lincoln and Lawrence H. Mamiya, *The Black Church in the African-American Experience* (Durham, N.C.: Duke University Press, 1990).

34. See chap. 1, n. 17.

35. For an introduction to feminist theology, see Barbara Brown Zikmund, "Theological Education as Advocate," *Theological Education* 25 (1988): 44-61, and "Ministry of Word and Sacrament: Women and Changing Understandings of Ordination," in *The Presbyterian Predicament,* pp. 134-58; Katie G. Cannon et al. (The Mud Flower Collective), *God's Fierce Whimsy: Christian Feminism and Theological Education* (New York: Pilgrim Press, 1985); The Cornwall Collective, *Your Daughters Shall Prophesy: Feminist Alternatives in Theological Education* (New York: Pilgrim Press, 1980); Rosemary Radford Ruether, "The Feminist Critique in Religious Studies," *Soundings* 64 (1981): 388-402, and "The Future of Feminist Theology in the Academy," *Journal of the American Academy of Religion* 53 (1985): 703-13. The best recent work in feminist theology is Elizabeth Johnson, *She Who Is: The Mystery of God in Feminist Theological Discourse* (New York: Crossroad, 1992).

36. Mulder and Wyatt, "The Predicament of Pluralism," in *The Pluralistic Vision,* pp. 37-70; *The Re-Forming Tradition,* p. 139; Van A. Harvey, "On the Intellectual Marginality of American Theology," in *Religion and Twentieth-Century American Intellectual Life,* ed. Michael J. Lacey (Cambridge: Cambridge University Press, 1989), pp. 172-92.

37. David J. Garrow, *Bearing the Cross: Martin Luther King, Jr. and the Southern Christian Leadership Conference* (New York: Morrow, 1986); James F. Findlay, *Church People in the Struggle: The National Council of Churches and the Black Freedom Movement, 1950–1970* (New York: Oxford University Press, 1993).

38. R. Douglas Brackenridge, *Eugene Carson Blake: Prophet with Portfolio* (New York: Seabury, 1978), p. 103; Joel L. Alvis, Jr., "A Presbyterian Dilemma: Ecclesiastical and Social Racial Policy in the Twentieth-Century Presbyterian Communion"; and Gayraud S. Wilmore, "Identity and Integration: Black Presbyterians and Their Allies in the Twentieth Century," in *The Diversity of Discipleship,* pp. 187-208, 209-34.

39. Robert N. Bellah, *The Broken Covenant: American Civil Religion in Time of Trial* (New York: Seabury Press, 1975); Ernest Lee Tuveson, *Redeemer Nation: The Idea of America's Millennial Role* (Chicago: University of Chicago Press, 1968); Frederick Merk, *Mission and Manifest Destiny in American History* (New York: Vintage Books, 1966).

40. David W. Levy, *The Debate over Vietnam* (Baltimore: Johns Hopkins University Press, 1991), pp. 93-97; Mitchell K. Hall, *Because of Their Faith: CALCAV and Religious Opposition to the Vietnam War* (New York: Columbia University Press, 1990); Rich L. Nutt, *Toward Peacemaking: Presbyterians in the South and National Security, 1945-1983* (Tuscaloosa: University of Alabama Press, 1994).

41. Ibid.

42. Bruce Grelle and David A. Krueger, eds., *Christianity and Capitalism* (Chicago: Center for the Scientific Study of Religion, 1986); Craig M. Gay, *With Liberty and Justice for Whom? The Recent Evangelical Debate over Capitalism* (Grand Rapids, Mich.: Wm. B. Eerdmans Publishing Co., 1991); J. Mark Thomas

and Vernon Visick, *God and Capitalism: A Prophetic Critique of Market Economy* (Madison, Wis.: A–R Editions, 1991); Michael Zweig, ed., *Religion and Economic Justice* (Philadelphia: Temple University Press, 1991); Timothy J. Gorringe, *Capital and Kingdom: Theological Ethics and the Economic Order* (Maryknoll, N.Y.: Orbis Books, 1994).

43. *Statistical Abstract of the United States,* 1963, p. 69; 1992, p. 93; George Barna, *The Future of the American Family* (Chicago: Moody Press, 1993), pp. 67-68; E. Brooks Holifield, "Pastoral Care and Counseling," in *Encyclopedia of the American Religious Experience,* pp. 1583-94; *A History of Pastoral Care in America: From Salvation to Self-Realization* (Nashville: Abingdon Press, 1983), pp. 210-356.

44. Nancy F. Cott, *The Grounding of Modern Feminism* (New Haven: Yale University Press, 1987); Carl Degler, *At Odds: Women and the Family in America from the Revolution to the Present* (New York: Oxford University Press, 1981). For two recent statements of feminist theology, see Rebecca Chopp, *The Power to Speak: Feminism, Language, God* (New York: Crossroad, 1990), and Johnson, *She Who Is.*

45. Bernard Asbell, *The Pill* (New York: Random House, 1995); Chopp, *The Power to Speak;* Maureen Muldoon, *The Abortion Debate in the United States and Canada* (New York: Garland, 1991); J. Gordon Melton, comp., *The Churches Speak on Abortion: Official Statements from Religious Bodies and Ecumenical Organizations* (Detroit: Gale Research, 1989).

46. Mark Ellingsen, "The Church and Abortion: Signs of Consensus," *The Christian Century* 107 (3 January 1990): 12-15; *Presbyterian Panel,* June 1988, p. 2.

47. *Presbyterian Panel,* June 1989, pp. 1-14, Appendix A.

48. *Detroit Free Press,* 15 July 1994; see also *Presbyterian Panel,* June 1989, pp. 9-14.

49. See Edward W. Farley, "The Presbyterian Heritage as Modernism: Reaffirming a Forgotten Past in Hard Times," in *The Presbyterian Predicament,* pp. 49-66.

Chapter 4

1. This chapter draws heavily on Milton J Coalter, John M. Mulder, and Louis B. Weeks, eds., *The Re-Forming Tradition: Presbyterians and Mainstream Protestantism* (Louisville, Ky.: Westminster/John Knox Press, 1992), pp. 199-222.

2. We are indebted to Charles Brockwell, our colleague and Methodist historian, for this description. See also Gerald O. McCulloh and Timothy L. Smith, "The Theology and Practice of Methodism, 1876–1919," in *The History of American Methodism,* 3 vols., ed. Emory Stevens Bucke (Nashville: Abingdon Press, 1964), 2:592-659.

3. See, e.g., Carolyn Atkins, "Menaul School: 1881–1930 . . . Not Leaders Merely, but Christian Leaders," *Journal of Presbyterian History* 58 (1980): 279-98.

4. James H. Smylie, " 'Of Secret and Family Worship': Historical Meditations, 1875–1975," *Journal of Presbyterian History* 58 (1980): 95-115.

5. Louis B. Weeks, "The Scriptures and Sabbath Observance in the South," *Journal of Presbyterian History* 59 (1981): 267-84.

6. Colleen McDannell, *The Christian Home in Victorian America, 1840–1900* (Bloomington, Ind.: Indiana University Press, 1986), p. 85.

7. Louis B. Weeks, "The Scriptures and Sabbath Observance in the South," *Journal of Presbyterian History* 58 (1980): 95-115; Benton Johnson, "On Dropping the Subject: Presbyterians and Sabbath Observance in the Twentieth Century," in *The Presbyterian Predicament: Six Perspectives,* ed. Milton J Coalter, John M. Mulder, and Louis B. Weeks (Louisville, Ky.: Westminster/John Knox Press, 1990), pp. 90-108.

8. Willard M. Swartley, *Slavery, Sabbath, War, and Women: Case Studies in Biblical Interpretation* (Scottdale, Pa.: Herald Press, 1983), pp. 67-96; R. J. Buckham, "Sabbath and Sunday in the Protestant Tradition," in *From Sabbath to Lord's Day: A Biblical, Historical, and Theological Investigation,* ed. D. A. Carson (Grand Rapids, Mich.: Zondervan, 1982), pp. 311-42.

9. Louis Weeks, *Kentucky Presbyterians* (Atlanta: John Knox Press, 1983), p. 11; Edward Bradford Davis, "Albert Barnes — 1798–1870: An Exponent of New School Presbyterianism" (Th.D. diss., Princeton Theological Seminary, 1961), pp. 357-69.

10. Johnson, "On Dropping the Subject," in *The Presbyterian Predicament,* pp. 90-108.

11. Robert W. Lynn and Elliott Wright, *The Big, Little School* (Nashville: Abingdon Press, 1980); Craig Dykstra and J. Bradley Wigger, "A Brief History of a Genre Problem: Presbyterian Educational Resource Materials," and David C. Hester, "The Use of the Bible in Presbyterian Curricula," in *The Pluralistic Vision: Presbyterians and Mainstream Protestant Education and Leadership,* ed. Milton J Coalter, John M. Mulder, and Louis B. Weeks (Louisville, Ky.: Westminster/John Knox Press, 1992), pp. 180-204, 205-34; Anne M. Boylan, *Sunday School: The Formation of an American Institution, 1790–1880* (New Haven: Yale University Press, 1988); Leonard I. Sweet, "Nineteenth-Century Evangelicalism," in *Encyclopedia of the American Religious Experience,* 3 vols., ed. Charles H. Lippy and Peter W. Williams (New York: Charles Scribner's Sons, 1988), 2:894-86.

12. Dale E. Soden, "Men and Mission: The Shifting Fortunes of Presbyterian Men's Organizations in the Twentieth Century," in *The Organizational Revolution: Presbyterians and American Denominationalism,* ed. Milton J Coalter, John M. Mulder, and Louis B. Weeks (Louisville, Ky.: Westminster/John Knox Press, 1992), pp. 233-53.

13. See n. 11; Dorothy Bass, "Ministry on the Margins: Protestants and Education," in *Between the Times: The Travail of the Protestant Establishment in*

America, 1900–1960, ed. William R. Hutchison (Cambridge: Cambridge University Press, 1989), pp. 48-71.

14. Ronald P. Byars, "Challenging the Ethos: A History of Presbyterian Worship Resources in the Twentieth Century," in *The Confessional Mosaic: Presbyterians and Twentieth-Century Theology,* ed. Milton J Coalter, John M. Mulder, and Louis B. Weeks (Louisville, Ky.: Westminster/John Knox Press, 1990), pp. 134-61; James F. White, "Liturgy and Worship," Paul Westermeyer, "Religious Music and Worship," and William B. Lawrence, "The History of Preaching in America," in *The Encyclopedia of the American Religious Experience,* pp. 1269-84, 1285-1306, 1307-24; Paul Westermeyer, "Twentieth-Century American Hymnody and Church Music," in *New Dimensions in American Religious History: Essays in Honor of Martin E. Marty,* ed. Jay P. Dolan and James P. Wind (Grand Rapids, Mich.: Wm. B. Eerdmans Publishing Co., 1993), pp. 175-208.

15. John McClure, "Changes in the Authority, Method, and Message of Presbyterian (UPCUSA) Preaching in the Twentieth Century," and Beverly Ann Zink, "Themes in Southern Presbyterian Preaching, 1920 to 1983," in *The Confessional Mosaic,* pp. 84-108, 109-33.

16. John M. Mulder, "The Heavenly City and Human Cities: Washington Gladden and Urban Reform," *Ohio History* 88 (1978): 151-74.

17. Morgan F. Simmons, "Hymnody: Its Place in Twentieth-Century Presbyterianism," in *The Confessional Mosaic,* p. 167; Linda J. Clark, " 'Songs My Mother Taught Me': Hymns as Transmitters of Faith," in *Beyond Establishment: Protestant Identity in a Post-Protestant Age,* ed. Jackson W. Carroll and Wade Clark Roof (Louisville, Ky.: Westminster/John Knox Press, 1993), pp. 99-115.

18. Ibid.; see also n. 15.

19. Quoted in McDannell, *The Christian Home in Victorian America,* p. 82.

20. "What a Friend We Have in Jesus" was composed ca. 1855 by Joseph Scriven for his mother; it was set to its familiar tune by Charles Crozat Converse in 1868. In addition to its popularity in the U.S., it has become a popular hymn for Korean Presbyterians. LindaJo H. McKim, *The Presbyterian Hymnal Companion* (Louisville, Ky.: Westminster/John Knox Press, 1993), pp. 280-81.

21. Louis Schneider and Sanford M. Dornbusch, *Popular Religion: Inspirational Books in America* (Chicago: University of Chicago Press, 1958).

22. "Light of the World, We Hail Thee" was composed in 1863 by John S. B. Monsell and was set to the tune of "Salve Domine" by Lawrence W. Watson in 1909. *The Hymnbook* (Richmond, Pa., and New York: Presbyterian Church in the United States, The United Presbyterian Church in the U.S.A., and the Reformed Church in America, 1955), p. 126.

23. Donald G. Tewksbury, *The Founding of American Colleges and Universities before the Civil War* (Hamden, Conn.: Archon Books, 1965); George M. Marsden, *The Soul of the American University: From Protestant Establishment to Established Nonbelief* (New York: Oxford University Press, 1994); Dorothy C. Bass, "Teaching With Authority: The Changing Place of Mainstream Protestantism in American Culture," in *Mainstream Protestantism in the Twentieth Century: Its*

Problems and Prospects (Louisville, Ky.: Committee on Theological Education, Presbyterian Church [USA], 1987), p. 5; Bradley J. Longfield and George M. Marsden, "Presbyterian Colleges in Twentieth-Century America," in *The Pluralistic Vision*, pp. 99-125; Douglas Sloan, *Faith and Knowledge: Mainline Protestantism and Higher Education* (Louisville, Ky.: Westminster/John Knox Press, 1994).

24. Ronald C. White, Jr., "Presbyterian Campus Ministries: Competing Loyalties and Changing Visions," in *The Pluralistic Vision*, pp. 126-47; Dorothy C. Bass, "Ministry on the Margins: Protestants and Education," in *Between the Times*, pp. 48-71.

25. Ibid.; Dorothy C. Bass, "Church-Related Colleges: Transmitters of Denominational Cultures?", Allison Stokes, "Denominational Ministry on University Campuses," and Louis B. Weeks, "Presbyterian Culture: Views from 'the Edge,'" in *Beyond Establishment*, pp. 157-72, 173-87, 309-26.

26. Mulder and Wyatt, "The Predicament of Pluralism," in *The Pluralistic Vision*, pp. 37-70; Steve Hancock, "Nurseries of Piety? Spiritual Formation at Four Presbyterian Seminaries," ibid., pp. 71-98; W. Clark Gilpin, "The Theological Schools: Transmission, Transformation, and Transcendence of Denominational Culture," in *Beyond Establishment*, pp. 188-204. For the patterns in the Disciples of Christ, see Mark A. Chaves, "The Changing Career Tracks of Elite Disciples Professionals," in *A Case Study of Mainstream Protestantism: The Disciples' Relation to American Culture, 1880–1989*, ed. D. Newell Williams (Grand Rapids, Mich.: Wm. B. Eerdmans Publishing Co., 1991), pp. 343-58; Edwin L. Becker, *Yale Divinity School and the Disciples of Christ, 1872–1989* (Nashville: Disciples Historical Society, 1990); Mark G. Toulouse, *Joined in Discipleship: The Maturing of an American Religious Movement* (St. Louis: Chalice Press, 1992), pp. 137-65.

27. Lawrence A. Cremin, *American Education: The National Experience, 1783-1876* (New York: Harper & Row, 1980).

28. Edwin S. Gaustad, "The Pulpit and the Pews," in *Between the Times*, p. 42.

29. Ibid.

30. John H. Westerhoff, *McGuffey and His Readers* (Nashville: Abingdon, 1978), p. 15.

31. F. Michael Perko, "Religious Education" and "Religious and Collegiate Education," in *Encyclopedia of the American Religious Experience*, pp. 1595-1610, 1611-26; Jay P. Dolan, *The American Catholic Experience* (Garden City, N.Y.: Doubleday, 1985), pp. 262-93; C. Eric Lincoln and Lawrence H. Mamiya, *The Black Church in the African American Experience* (Durham, N.C.: Duke University Press, 1990), pp. 251-53; Nathan Glazer, *American Judaism*, 2nd ed. (Chicago: University of Chicago Press, 1972), pp. 71-73, 85-87, 109-13, 119-21, 158-59.

32. C. Howard Hopkins, *History of the YMCA in North America* (New York: Association Press, 1951), and *John R. Mott: 1865–1955: A Biography* (Grand Rapids, Mich.: Wm. B. Eerdmans Publishing Co., 1979); Grace H. Wilson, *The Religious and Educational Philosophy of the Young Women's Christian Association* (New York: Bureau of Publications, Teachers College, Columbia University, 1933).

33. See n. 32; Robert H. Bremner, *American Philanthropy* (Chicago: University of Chicago Press, 1960), pp. 122-86.

34. See n. 13; see also Don S. and Carol Browning, "The Church and the Family Crisis: A New Love Ethic," *Christian Century* 108 (7 August 1991): 746-49; Ellen T. Charry, "Raising Christian Children in a Pagan Culture," *Christian Century* 111 (16 February 1994): 166-68; Barbara Dafoe Whitehead, "Dan Quayle Was Right," *Atlantic Monthly* 271 (April 1993): 47-84.

35. Peter L. Benson and Carolyn H. Eklin, *Effective Christian Education: A National Study of Protestant Congregations: A Summary Report on Faith, Loyalty and Congregational Life* (Minneapolis: Search Institute, 1990), p. 46.

36. Marian Wright Edelman, "Leave No Child Behind," *Church and Society* 84 (1993): 135.

37. Benton Johnson, "From Old to New Agendas: Presbyterians and Social Issues in the Twentieth Century," in *The Confessional Mosaic,* pp. 208-35.

38. See n. 34. See also Penny Long Marler, "Lost in the Fifties: The Changing Family and the Nostalgic Church," in *Work, Family, and Religion in American Society,* ed. Nancy T. Ammerman and Wade Clark Roof (New York: Routledge, 1995).

39. John B. Trotti and Richard A. Ray, "Presbyterians and Their Publishing Houses," in *The Pluralistic Vision,* pp. 148-79; James H. Moorhead, "Redefining Confessionalism: American Presbyterians in the Twentieth Century," in *The Confessional Mosaic,* pp. 63-64.

40. Craig Dykstra and J. Bradley Wigger, "A Brief History of a Genre Problem: Presbyterian Educational Resource Materials," in *The Pluralistic Vision,* p. 192; David C. Hester, "The Use of the Bible in Presbyterian Curricula, 1923–1985," in ibid., pp. 205-34.

41. Ibid.

42. *Holland* (Mich.) *Sentinel,* 25 July 1994.

43. Benton Johnson, "On Dropping the Subject: Presbyterians and Sabbath Observance in the Twentieth Century," in *The Presbyterian Predicament,* pp. 90-108.

44. Francis J. Sorauf, *The Wall of Separation* (Princeton: Princeton University Press, 1976); John F. Wilson, ed., *Church and State in America: A Bibliographical Guide* (New York: Greenwood Press, 1986–87); Glenn Miller, "Church and State," in *Encyclopedia of the American Religious Experience,* pp. 1369-92.

45. Longfield and Marsden, "Presbyterian Colleges in Twentieth-Century America," in *The Pluralistic Vision,* pp. 99-126; Marsden, *The Soul of the American University;* Marsden and Longfield, eds., *The Secularization of the Academy* (New York: Oxford University Press, 1992); Bass, "Ministry on the Margin," in *Between the Times,* pp. 48-71.

46. Ibid.

47. Robert Wuthnow, *The Restructuring of American Religion: Society and Faith Since World War II* (Princeton: Princeton University Press, 1988), p. 155; Bass, "Ministry on the Margin," in *Between the Times,* p. 49.

48. Coalter, Mulder, and Weeks, *The Re-Forming Tradition,* p. 159.

49. Wuthnow, *The Restructuring of American Religion,* pp. 157-64; James Davison Hunter, *Evangelicalism: The Coming Generation* (Chicago: University of Chicago Press, 1987), pp. 165-78.

50. Dean R. Hoge, Benton Johnson, and Donald A. Luidens, *Vanishing Boundaries: The Religion of Mainline Protestant Baby Boomers* (Louisville, Ky.: Westminster/John Knox Press, 1994), p. 169.

51. See n. 45.

52. Robert Wuthnow, "How Small Groups Are Transforming Our Lives," and Warren Bird, "The Great Small-Group Takeover," *Christianity Today* 38 (7 February 1994): 20-24, 25-29; Robert Wuthnow, *Sharing the Journey* (New York: Free Press, 1994).

53. Ibid.

54. Wuthnow, "How Small Groups are Transforming Our Lives," p. 24.

55. Robert Wuthnow, ed., *"I Come Away Stronger": How Small Groups Are Changing American Religion* (Grand Rapids, Mich.: Wm. B. Eerdmans Publishing Co., 1994).

56. Wuthnow, "How Small Groups Are Transforming Our Lives," and *Sharing the Journey.*

57. Gary S. Eller, "Special Interest-Groups and American Presbyterianism," in *The Denominational Revolution,* pp. 100-131, and Robert Wuthnow, "The Restructuring of American Presbyterianism: Turmoil in One Denomination," in *The Presbyterian Predicament,* pp. 27-48. William McKinney of Hartford Seminary provided the list of UCC single-issue groups.

58. Ibid.

Chapter 5

1. Peter Drucker, *The New Realities: In Government and Politics, in Economics and Society, in Business, Technology, and World View* (New York: Harper & Row, 1989), p. 3.

2. Winthrop S. Hudson, "Denominationalism as a Basis for Ecumenicity: A Seventeenth Century Conception," in *Denominationalism,* ed. Russell E. Richey (Nashville: Abingdon Press, 1977), pp. 21-49.

3. Sydney Ahlstrom, *A Religious History of the American People* (New Haven: Yale University Press, 1972), pp. 379-83.

4. William R. Hutchison, *Errand to the World: American Protestant Thought and Foreign Missions* (Chicago: University of Chicago Press, 1987); R. Pierce Beaver, "Missionary Motivation through Three Centuries," in *Reinterpretation in American Church History,* ed. Jerald C. Brauer (Chicago: University of Chicago Press, 1968), pp. 113-52.

5. Charles I. Foster, *An Errand of Mercy: The Evangelical United Front,*

1790–1837 (Chapel Hill, N.C.: University of North Carolina Press, 1960); John W. Kuykendall, *The Southern Enterprise: The Work of National Evangelical Societies in the Antebellum South* (Westport, Conn.: Greenwood Press, 1982).

6. E. Brooks Holifield, "Toward a History of American Congregations," in *American Congregations,* vol. 2: *New Perspectives in the Study of Congregations,* ed. James P. Wind and James W. Lewis (Chicago: University of Chicago Press, 1994), pp. 23-53.

7. Kenneth Scott Latourette, *The Great Century, 1800–1914,* vols. 4-6 in *A History of Christianity,* 7 vols. (New York: Harper & Bros., 1938–46).

8. Joan C. LaFollette, "Money and Power: Presbyterian Women's Organizations in the Twentieth Century," in *The Organizational Revolution,* ed. Milton J Coalter, John M. Mulder, and Louis B. Weeks (Louisville, Ky.: Westminster/John Knox Press, 1992), p. 212; Coalter, Mulder, and Weeks, eds., *The Re-Forming Tradition: Presbyterians and Mainstream Protestantism* (Louisville, Ky.: Westminster/John Knox Press, 1992), p. 167.

9. Quoted in Robert T. Handy, *A Christian America: Protestant Hopes and Historical Realties,* 2nd ed. (New York: Charles Scribner's Sons, 1986), p. 106.

10. Hutchison, *Errand to the World,* pp. 77-90.

11. Ibid., pp. 43-90.

12. Craig Dykstra and James Hudnut-Beumler, "The National Structures of Protestant Denominations: An Invitation to a Conversation," in *The Organizational Revolution,* pp. 307-32.

13. Louis B. Weeks, "The Incorporation of the Presbyterians," in ibid., pp. 37-54; Robert H. Wiebe, *The Search for Order, 1877–1920* (New York: Hill & Wang, 1967); Alan Trachtenberg, *The Incorporation of America: Culture and Society in the Gilded Age* (New York: Hill and Wang, 1982).

14. Weeks, "The Incorporation of the Presbyterians"; Coalter, Mulder, and Weeks, *The Re-Forming Tradition,* pp. 91-116.

15. Coalter, Mulder, and Weeks, *The Re-Forming Tradition,* pp. 91-116.

16. Ibid.

17. Paul M. Harrison, *Authority and Power in the Free Church Tradition* (Princeton: Princeton University Press, 1959), p. 45.

18. Ibid., pp. 42-43, 48-49.

19. James Overbeck, "The Rise and Fall of Presbyterian Official Journals, 1925–1985," in *The Diversity of Discipleship,* ed. Milton J Coalter, John M. Mulder, and Louis B. Weeks (Louisville, Ky.: Westminster/John Knox Press, 1991), pp. 83-104; Theodore A. Gill, Jr., "American Presbyterians in the Global Ecumenical Movement," in ibid., pp. 126-48; Erskine Clarke, "Presbyterian Ecumenical Activity in the United States," in ibid., pp. 149-69.

20. Robert Bruce Mullin and Russell E. Richey, eds., *Reimagining Denominationalism: Interpretive Essays* (New York: Oxford University Press, 1994); Martin E. Marty, "Denominations: Can't Live with 'Em, Can't Live without 'Em," *Christian Century* 111 (7 December 1994): 1159-65.

21. John R. Fitzmier and Randall Balmer, "A Poultice for the Bite of the

Cobra: The Hocking Report and Presbyterian Missions in the Middle Decades of the Twentieth Century," in *Reimagining Denominationalism,* pp. 105-9; Hutchison, *Errand to the World,* pp. 158-83.

22. Fitzmier and Balmer, "A Poultice for the Bite of the Cobra," in *Reimagining Denominationalism,* pp. 109-23.

23. Hutchison, *Errand to the World,* pp. 176-202; Emerito P. Nacpil, "Mission but Not Missionaries," *International Review of Mission* 60 (1971): 356-62.

24. Grant Wacker, "A Plural World: The Protestant Awakening to World Religions," in *Between the Times: The Travail of the Protestant Establishment in America, 1900–1960,* ed. William R. Hutchison (Cambridge: Cambridge University Press, 1989), p. 263.

25. Gayraud S. Wilmore, "Identity and Integration: Black Presbyterians and Their Allies in the Twentieth Century," in *The Diversity of Discipleship,* pp. 209-33; Henry Warner Bowden, "Native-American Presbyterians: Assimilation, Leadership, and Future Challenges," in ibid., pp. 234-56; Francisco O. Garcia-Treto and R. Douglas Brackenridge, "Hispanic Presbyterians: Life in Two Cultures," in ibid., pp. 257-79; Michael J. Kimura Angevine and Ryo Yoshida, "Contexts for a History of Asian American Presbyterian Churches: A Case Study of the Early History of Japanese American Presbyterians," in ibid., pp. 280-311; Sang Hyun Lee, "Korean American Presbyterians: A Need for Ethnic Particularity and the Challenge of Christian Pilgrimage," in ibid., pp. 312-30; George E. Tinker, *Missionary Conquest: The Gospel and Native American Cultural Genocide* (Minneapolis: Fortress Press, 1993).

26. Ibid.

27. Ibid.

28. Catherine M. Prelinger, *Episcopal Women: Gender, Spirituality, and Commitment in an American Mainline Denomination* (New York: Oxford University Press, 1992); Elizabeth H. Verdesi, *In but Still Out: Women in the Church* (Philadelphia: Westminster Press, 1972); Virginia Lieson Brereton, "United and Slighted: Women as Subordinated Insiders," in Hutchison, ed., *Between the Times,* pp. 143-67; Joan C. LaFollette, "Money and Power: Presbyterian Women's Organizations in the Twentieth Century," in *The Organizational Revolution,* pp. 199-232; Edward C. Lehmann, *Women Clergy: Breaking through Gender Barriers* (New Brunswick, N.J.: Transaction Books, 1985), and *Gender and Work: The Case of the Clergy* (Albany: State University of New York Press, 1993).

29. James Hudnut-Beumler, *Looking for God in the Suburbs: The Religion of the American Dream and Its Critics* (New Brunswick, N.J.: Rutgers University Press, 1994); Robert N. Bellah et al., *The Good Society* (New York: Alfred A. Knopf, 1991), pp. 3-18, 62-64.

30. See the studies by Richard W. Reifsnyder, "Changing Leadership Patterns in the Presbyterian Church in the United States during the Twentieth Century," "Transformations in Administrative Leadership in the United Presbyterian Church in the U.S.A., 1920–1983," and "Looking for Leadership: The

Emerging Style of Leadership in the Presbyterian Church (U.S.A.), 1983–1990," in *The Pluralistic Vision,* ed. Coalter, Mulder, and Weeks (Louisville, Ky.: Westminster/John Knox Press, 1992), pp. 235-88; Reifsnyder, "Managing the Mission: Church Restructuring in the Twentieth Century," in *The Organizational Revolution,* pp. 37-54; Mark A. Chaves, "The Changing Career Tracks of Elite Disciples Professionals," in *A Case Study of Mainstream Protestantism: The Disciples' Relation to American Culture: 1880–1980,* ed. D. Newell Williams (Grand Rapids, Mich.: Wm. B. Eerdmans Publishing Co., 1991), pp. 343-58; Mark Chaves, "Denominations as Dual Structures: An Organizational Analysis," *Sociology of Religion* 54 (1993): 147-69.

31. Benton Johnson, "From Old to New Agendas: Presbyterians and Social Issues in the Twentieth Century," in *The Confessional Mosaic,* ed. Coalter, Mulder, and Weeks (Louisville, Ky.: Westminster/John Knox Press, 1990), pp. 208-35.

32. Louis B. Weeks and William Fogleman, "A Two-Church Hypothesis," *Presbyterian Outlook* 172 (26 March 1990): 8; see also Keith M. Wulff and John P. Marcum, "Cleavage or Consensus? A New Look at the Clergy-Laity Gap," in *The Pluralistic Vision,* pp. 308-26.

33. Lewis L. Wilkins, "The American Presbytery in the Twentieth Century," in *The Organizational Revolution,* pp. 96-121; Dykstra and Hudnut-Beumler, "The National Organizational Structures of Protestant Denominations," in ibid., p. 308; Reifsnyder, "Managing the Mission," in ibid., pp. 66-95.

34. Donald A. Luidens and Roger J. Nemath, "Congregational vs. Denominational Giving: An Analysis of Giving Patterns in The Presbyterian Church in the United States and the Reformed Church in America," *Review of Religious Research* 36 (1994): 111-22; Scott Brunger and Robin Klay, "A Financial History of American Presbyterian Giving," in *The Organizational Revolution,* pp. 122-31.

35. Ibid. See also Robin Klay, "Changing Priorities: Allocation of Giving in the Presbyterian Church in the U.S.," in *The Organization Revolution,* pp. 132-53; Scott Brunger, "Global and Local Mission: Allocation of Giving in the Presbyterian Church in the U.S.A. and the United Presbyterian Church in the U.S.A., 1923–1982," in ibid., pp. 154-70; D. Scott Cormode, "A Financial History of Presbyterian Congregations Since World War II," in ibid., pp. 171-98.

36. Ibid.; John and Sylvia Ronsvalle, "The State of Church Giving Through 1991," in *Yearbook of American and Canadian Churches, 1994,* ed. Kenneth B. Bedell (Nashville: Abingdon Press, 1990), pp. 12-16.

37. *Minutes of the General Assembly of the Presbyterian Church (USA), 1990* (Louisville, Ky., 1990), p. 536; see also the articles by Scott Brunger, Robin Klay, and D. Scott Cormode in *The Organizational Revolution,* pp. 122-98.

38. Reifsnyder, "Managing the Mission," in *The Organizational Revolution,* pp. 55-96.

39. Joel A. Carpenter and Wilbert R. Shenk, eds., *Earthen Vessels: American Evangelicals and Foreign Missions, 1880–1980* (Grand Rapids, Mich.: Wm. B. Eerdmans Publishing Co., 1990), p. xii.

40. W. Dayton Roberts and John A. Siewert, eds., *Mission Handbook*, 14th ed. (Grand Rapids, Mich.: Zondervan, 1989), p. 54.

41. We are indebted to Darrell L. Guder of Louisville Seminary for this information; see also *The NonProfit Times*, November 1994, p. 35.

42. Nancy T. Ammerman, "SBC Moderates and the Making of a Postmodern Denomination," *Christian Century* 110 (22 September 1993): 896-99.

Chapter 6

1. See also Tony Campolo, *Can Mainline Denominations Make a Comeback?* (Valley Forge, Pa.: Judson Press, 1995); C. Kirk Hadaway and David A. Roozen, *Rerouting the Protestant Mainstream: Sources of Growth and Opportunities for Change* (Nashville: Abingdon, 1995).

2. *Monday Morning*, June 1994, p. 10.

3. See, e.g., Ruth H. Bloch, *Visionary Republic: Millennial Themes in American Thought, 1756–1800* (New York: Cambridge University Press, 1985), "Religion and Ideological Change in the American Revolution," in *Religion and American Politics: From the Colonial Period to the 1980s*, ed. Mark A. Noll (New York: Oxford University Press, 1990), pp. 44-63; Nathan O. Hatch, *The Sacred Cause of Liberty: Republican Thought and the Millennium in Revolutionary New England* (New Haven: Yale University Press, 1977); Alan Heimert, *Religion and the American Mind from the Great Awakening to the Revolution* (Cambridge: Harvard University Press, 1966); Perry Miller, "From the Covenant to the Revival," in *Nature's Nation* (Cambridge: Harvard University Press, 1967); Edmund S. Morgan, "The Puritan Ethic and the American Revolution," *William and Mary Quarterly*, 3rd series, 24 (1967): 3-43.

4. See, e.g., Donald G. Mathews, "The Second Great Awakening as an Organizing Process, 1780–1830," *American Quarterly* 21 (1969): 29-43; Nathan O. Hatch, "The Democratization of Christianity and the Character of American Politics," in *Religion and American Politics*, pp. 92-120; *The Democratization of American Christianity* (New Haven: Yale University Press, 1989).

5. William G. McLoughlin, *Revivals, Awakenings, and Reform: An Essay on Religious and Social Change in America, 1607–1977* (Chicago: University of Chicago Press, 1978); Robert S. Ellwood, *The Sixties: American Religion Moving from Modern to Postmodern* (New Brunswick, N.J.: Rutgers University Press, 1994).

6. This theme is developed at greater length in "The Presbyterian Predicament: A Case of Conflicting Allegiances," in *The Re-Forming Tradition*, ed. Milton J Coalter, John M. Mulder, and Louis B. Weeks (Louisville, Ky.: Westminster/John Knox Press, 1992), pp. 225-44.

7. For a striking example of the persistence of denial, see Starr Luteri, "Be Kind to Mainline Churches," *Current Issues*, Adult Foundational Curriculum

(Louisville: Presbyterian Publishing House, 1993). In his introduction, editor Frank Hainer observes: "But maybe nothing has 'happened.' Things are different from the way they were in the fifties, it is true, but maybe the fifties were the aberration and things are just getting back to normal" (p. 4).

8. John Calvin, *Institutes of the Christian Religion*, ed. John T. McNeill, and trans. Ford Lewis Battles (Philadelphia: Westminster Press, 1960), 1.7.4-5.

9. Robert McAfee Brown, *The Spirit of Protestantism* (New York: Oxford University Press, 1961), pp. 79-80.

10. Coalter, Mulder, and Weeks, *The Re-Forming Tradition*, pp. 250-53.

11. "Characteristics of the American Presbyterian, prepared for the PC(USA), April 26, 1984," Simmons Market Research Bureau. We are indebted to Keith Wulff of the Presbyterian Church (USA) Research Office for this reference.

12. "Two Surveys of the Unchurched" (Louisville: Research Services, Presbyterian Church [U.S.A.], n.d.).

13. See, for example, the essays on African American, Native American, Hispanic, Japanese American, and Korean American Presbyterians by Joel Alvis, Gayraud S. Wilmore, Henry Warner Bowden, Francisco O. Garcia-Treto and R. Douglas Brackenridge, Michael J. Kimura Angevine and Ryo Yoshida, and Sang Hyun Lee in *The Diversity of Discipleship*, ed. Milton J Coalter, John M. Mulder, and Louis B. Weeks (Louisville, Ky.: Westminster/John Knox Press, 1991), pp. 170-311.

14. Penny Long Marler and C. Kirk Hadaway, "New Church Development and Denominational Growth (1950-1988): Symptom or Cause?" in *Church and Denominational Growth*, ed. David A. Roozen and C. Kirk Hadaway (Nashville: Abingdon, 1993), p. 51.

15. Ibid., p. 51.

16. Ibid., pp. 85-86.

17. Marler and Hadaway, "New Church Development and Denominational Growth," p. 86.

18. Coalter, Mulder, and Weeks, *The Re-Forming Tradition*, pp. 258-60.

19. Ibid.; Robert N. Bellah et al., *Habits of the Heart: Individualism and Commitment in American Life* (New York: Harper & Row, 1985), pp. 56-65.

20. *The Presbyterian Hymnal: Hymns, Psalms, and Spiritual Songs* (Louisville: Westminster/John Knox Press, 1990), 441.

21. Martin E. Marty, *Modern American Religion: The Noise of Conflict*.

22. For an insightful analysis of this issue, see Barbara Brown Zikmund, "The Values and Limits of Representation and Pluralism in the Church," in *The Pluralistic Vision*, ed. Milton J Coalter, John M. Mulder, and Louis B. Weeks (Westminster/John Knox Press, 1992), pp. 327-48.

23. James Davison Hunter, *Culture Wars: The Struggle to Define America* (New York: Basic Books, 1991); David Harrington Watt, *A Transforming Faith: Explorations in Twentieth-Century American Evangelicalism* (New Brunswick, N.J.: Rutgers University Press, 1991).

24. Dean R. Hoge, Benton Johnson, and Donald A. Luidens, *Vanishing*

Boundaries: The Religion of Mainline Protestant Baby Boomers (Louisville, Ky.: Westminster/John Knox Press, 1994), pp. 179-80.

25. Paul Tillich, *The Protestant Era* (Chicago: University of Chicago Press, 1948), pp. 161-84.

26. See, for example, Rogers and McKim, "Presbyterian Views of Scripture," in *The Confessional Mosaic,* ed. Milton J Coalter, John M. Mulder, and Louis B. Weeks (Louisville, Ky.: Westminster/John Knox Press, 1990), pp. 49-58; and Jack Rogers, *Claiming the Center: Churches and Conflicting World Views* (Louisville, Ky.: Westminster/John Knox Press, 1995).

27. Coalter, Mulder, and Weeks, *The Re-Forming Tradition,* pp. 264-67; Grayson L. Tucker, "Enhancing Church Vitality Through Congregational Identity Change," in *The Mainstream Protestant "Decline,"* ed. Milton J Coalter, John M. Mulder, and Louis B. Weeks (Louisville, Ky.: Westminster/John Knox Press, 1990), pp. 66-85; Mark Wilhelm, "The New Voluntarism and Presbyterian Affiliation," in ibid., pp. 150-76; Stephen Warner, "Mirror for American Protestantism: Mendocino Presbyterian Church in the Sixties and Seventies," in ibid., pp. 198-224. For a survey of how congregations might serve as the focus for analyzing contemporary American Protestantism, see Barbara G. Wheeler, "Uncharted Territory: Congregational Identity and Mainline Protestantism," in *The Presbyterian Predicament,* ed. Coalter, Mulder, and Weeks (Louisville, Ky.: Westminster/John Knox Press, 1990), pp. 67-89.

28. *Holland* (Mich.) *Sentinel,* 17 August 1991.

29. Coalter, Mulder, and Weeks, *The Re-Forming Tradition,* pp. 281-87.

30. Roof and McKinney, *American Mainline Religion,* p. 242; their italics.

31. Lesslie Newbigin, *Foolishness to the Greeks* (Grand Rapids, Mich.: Wm. B. Eerdmans Publishing Co., 1989), pp. 1-20.

32. George Gallup, Jr., and Jim Castelli, *The People's Religion: American Faith in the 1990s* (New York: Macmillan, 1989), pp. 3-21.

33. Wade Clark Roof, *A Generation of Seekers: The Spiritual Journeys of the Baby Boom Generation* (San Francisco: Harper, 1993).

34. Leander E. Keck, *The Church Confident* (Nashville: Abingdon, 1993), pp. 27, 30, 33.

35. H. Richard Niebuhr, *Faith on Earth,* p. 66, quoted in Keck, *The Church Confident,* p. 30.

36. Donald A. Luidens, Dean R. Hoge, and Benton Johnson, "The Emergence of Lay Liberalism Among Baby Boomers," *Theology Today* 51 (1994): 253.

37. Coalter, Mulder, and Weeks, *The Re-Forming Tradition,* pp. 281-87.

38. Benton Johnson, Dean R. Hoge, and Donald A. Luidens, "Mainline Churches: The Real Reason for Decline," *First Things* 31 (1993): 18.

Index

161